AN
ILLUSTRATED
HISTORY OF
TRANSPORT

AN
ILLUSTRATED
HISTORY OF
TRANSPORT

Anthony Ridley

HEINEMANN : LONDON

William Heinemann Ltd
15 Queen St, Mayfair, London W1X 8BE
LONDON MELBOURNE TORONTO
JOHANNESBURG AUCKLAND

First published in Great Britain 1969
Copyright © 1969 Anthony Ridley
Reprinted 1972, 1976

434 63720 3

Printed and bound in Great Britain by
Cox & Wyman Ltd,
London, Fakenham and Reading

Contents

I

From Prehistory to 500 B.C.

Man is a toolmaker and a traveller. Even the earliest known manlike creatures of some million years ago made crude weapons to kill their animal prey. Modern man's remote forefathers were fierce hunters and probably followed the great herds of grazing animals, killing those they needed for food. If rivers blocked their path, the hunters waded or swam across until eventually they learned to hold onto floating branches to support themselves in the water. This was the beginning of the boat, man's first vehicle.

Our knowledge of subsequent developments in transport up to Neolithic (or New Stone Age) times, c. 6000 B.C., is largely the result of intelligent guesswork. Even the archaeologists can tell us very little. For thousands of years, floating tree trunks were probably used to support swimmers. Some of them learned to climb astride the trunk and paddle with their hands. Perhaps it was one of these trunk riders who cleverly thought of using a flat piece of wood as a more effective paddle than his own limbs.

Time went on, and further improvements were made. Some men fashioned rafts by tying logs together. Others made dugout canoes from whole tree trunks hollowed out after having been softened with hot water or partially burned away by fire. Man was learning to travel more comfortably and safely on the water.

These modern dugout canoes have changed little from those used by early man.

1

Sledges were the first land vehicles. The forest dwellers of Neolithic Europe became skilled at working wood. Wooden runners of the sledges which they pulled 8,000 years ago still survive, preserved in the peat of Danish swamps.

These Neolithic woodworkers were still nomadic hunters and food-gatherers when, in the Middle East, a way of life which would eventually revolutionize the world was developing. Man was learning to sow cereals and breed domestic animals, like the sheep and the goat. In especially fertile and well-watered areas, man began to establish permanent farming settlements. Settled conditions allowed communities to produce surplus food so that experts, like potters and flintworkers, could practise their skills full time and sell their wares to earn their daily bread.

Even in Neolithic times there was irregular trading among the farming villages of the Middle East, and this trade required transport. Commerce was probably at first mainly confined to settlements linked by rivers or streams, since boats or rafts could glide easily along the waterways. Overland transport by sledge must have been a very different matter. Every bump must have tended to upset the load, while the friction of the sledge's runners over rough ground must have made pulling difficult.

As civilization advanced, man had to shift heavier and heavier objects. Great slabs of rock were needed to build temples and shrines, and these huge loads had to be moved somehow from the quarries to the chosen sites. Sledges could be used only when an immense labour force was available, but someone must have noticed how easily a felled tree would trundle down a hillside once its branches were lopped off. This led to the idea of log rollers. A massive rock would be laid on a number of well-shaped logs. Ropes would be tied around it, and gangs of men would haul it forward over the turning rollers. As each roller was in turn left behind, it would be moved to the front again so that it could be used once more.

Of course, the labour of moving the rollers which were left behind made them too cumbersome for light loads. Perhaps the next stage of development was a rough plank cart, with a log roller fixed permanently underneath between two pairs of wooden pegs. Such roller carts would have been an improvement on sledges but still would have been hard to push when loaded because of the way the roller rubbed against the underside of the planks as it turned.

During the fifth millenium B.C., when the first great civilizations of which much is known began to emerge in Egypt and Mesopotamia, men were using rafts or dugout canoes on water, while on land they dragged heavy loads on rollers and sledges and carried lighter goods on roller carts and pack

A reconstruction of transportation in ancient Egypt. On land, heavy loads were hauled along by teams of straining labourers, but on water the use of sail had already lightened the burden of work.

animals. In all probability, cultures had reached the same level in India and China by that time.

The Egyptian civilization was centred on the Nile, and Mesopotamia was watered by two great rivers, the Tigris and the Euphrates, so both peoples must have used boats from their earliest days. Practically nothing has been discovered about the larger Mesopotamian ships, but in Egypt the warm, dry climate has preserved the archaeological remains, so that carvings, models and wall paintings of ships have survived to the present day.

Big trees have always been rare in Egypt, so dugout canoes could not be made. Instead, the early boatbuilders on the Nile used materials which were plentiful and close at hand and built rafts from bundles of river reeds. These rafts floated well when launched, but they quickly became waterlogged. The Egyptians also built genuine boats by joining together innumerable small pieces of wood, which were all that could be cut from the tiny acacia trees of their country. Craftsmen carefully shaped each miniature plank and bored holes at the edges so that they could tie neighbouring timbers together with thongs. These ships were sewn up almost like a suit of clothes, and reeds were squashed into the gaps between planks to prevent leaks.   3

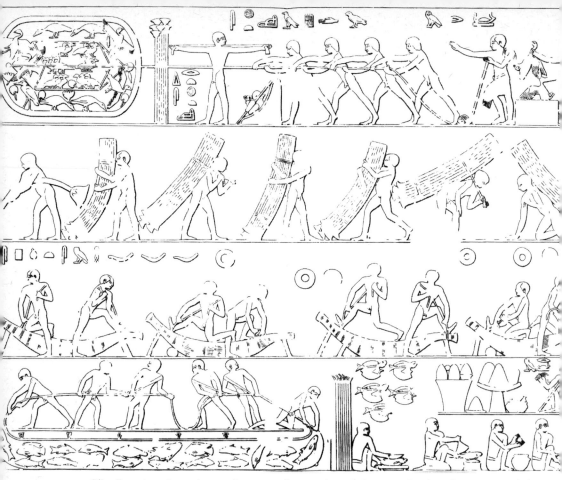

The Egyptians learned to make canoes from rushes, their most abundant buoyant material. This illustration, taken from a wall painting of about 2600 B.C., shows such a canoe being built.

Later the Egyptians discovered how to make stronger boats by joining timbers together with wooden pegs.

It is quite possible that the Egyptians were the first people to use sails. From the earliest times, the Nile River was crowded with all kinds of ships, and before long it must have been noticed how the wind, which nearly always blew upstream, helped the oarsmen against the current. Probably they took the logical step and learned to catch more wind in a spread of cloth. Of course, the Egyptians could not have used the wind when descending the Nile, but, then, they would hardly have needed it with the flow of water to help them.

At first the Egyptians kept to the sheltered Nile, which ran the length of their country, but shortages slowly forced them to venture out into the Mediterranean. Often the quest was for building timber, while sometimes expeditions were fitted out to search for the firs and junipers from which came the oils and resins needed for embalming the dead. In *c.* 2700 B.C. the

Pharaoh Snefru sent out a fleet of sixty ships, some of which were 150 feet long, on such a mission. They crept along the coast to Syria and traded successfully for resinous trees.

Two hundred years later, another Pharaoh, Sahu-re, sent out a large expedition to bring back timber. A tomb carving of one of his ships has survived, so a good deal is known about how they looked. Instead of being single poles, their masts were shaped like capital *A*'s, and their hulls were made of fairly small pieces of shaped wood sewn together with tough thongs. When these outer skins had been built, ribs were fitted to keep the hulls in shape, but even with the ribs, Sahu-re's ships were weak. They would certainly have broken up in rough weather without the thick rope which ran above deck from bow to stern in each boat. Strong ropes stretched around the upper part of each hull kept the timbers in place and also served as fenders. The ships were propelled by both oars and sails.

Sculptures survive of another great expedition sent out more than 1,000 years later, in about 1500 B.C. Luxury goods, like ivory, frankincense, and gold, had been reaching Egypt overland from the distant and mysterious country of Punt, which lay somewhere south of the Red Sea. The trade had

Seagoing ships from a relief in the pyramid tomb of Sahu-re, c. 2500 B.C.
The peculiar A-shaped masts have been lowered.

passed through so many hands that prices had become outrageous, and the ruler of the day, Queen Hatshepsut, decided that the solution was for the Egyptians to find their own way to the land of Punt by sea. A fleet was fitted out, and it sailed the entire length of the Red Sea, passing through the narrow mouth into the unknown. The ships probably then made their way along the coast of modern Somalia and may even have crossed to Arabia. The

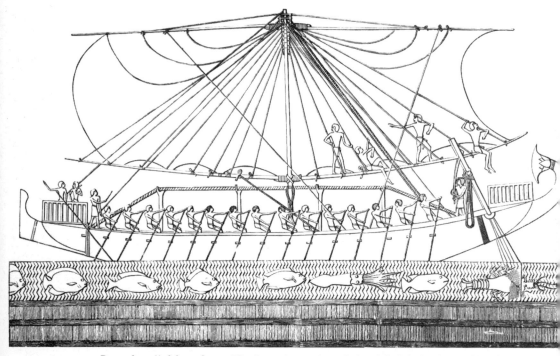

Part of a relief from Queen Hatshepsut's temple at Deier el Bahri showing a ship which took part in her expedition to Punt, c. 1500 B.C.

expedition was successful beyond anyone's wildest hopes, and the boats came home bulging with gold, ivory, and Negro slaves. Even so, a little space was spared for such startling animals as the giraffe, which were taken to amuse and surprise the queen. Hatshepsut was delighted and proclaimed that there had never been an expedition like this one from the beginning of time.

Ass-drawn Mesopotamian chariots from the "standard" of Ur,
c. 2750 B.C.

Later in her reign, Hatshepsut decorated a temple with sculptures commemorating the voyage to Punt. These still exist and show just what her ships looked like. The hulls were almost unchanged from Sahu-re's time 1,000 years before, but the rigging was very different. Masts had become single poles mounted amidships instead of nearer the bow, while sails had grown wider and bigger. Since sailcloth was still not very strong, the bottoms of these large sails had to be strengthened by wooden booms, supported by ropes spreading out from higher up on the masts. Like their predecessors, Hatshepsut's boats were guided by steering oars, but there had been improvements. The oars were no longer just held over the side near the stern. Now they were permanently fixed into position, one on each side of the ship, and they were connected to the same tiller.

Egypt's slow mastery of the water was matched elsewhere by the invention of the wheel for use on land. The origin of the wheel is uncertain, but it seems probable that the first wheels were disks cut out of tree trunks. Nevertheless, most archeologists agree that it would have been difficult to hack out even such simple shapes except with the most perfect of stone tools, and it seems likely that wheels were not made before men had learned to work with metal at the beginning of the Middle Eastern Bronze Age about 6,000 years ago.

The use of the wheel spread, and it was common throughout Mesopotamia by 3000 B.C. At approximately this time, its military possibilities must have been realized, for mosaic pictures of war chariots appear on a standard dating from 2750 B.C. which was found on the site of the ancient Mesopotamian city of Ur. Each of these chariots had four solid wheels and was drawn by two asses. Two men were carried, one drove, and the other was a warrior

7

armed with javelins. By 2500 B.C. the wheel and probably the chariot had spread still farther afield and had reached both Egypt and western India.

War chariots had to be fast and reliable, so that heavy solid wheels, which might easily split in two when the going became rough, were far from ideal. In about 2000 B.C. the men of Mesopotamia invented the spoked wheel, which was both lighter and stronger, and from then on, solid wheels were used only for their farm wagons.

At the time when the secret of the wheel was slowly spreading out from Mesopotamia, Stone Age farmers along the river valleys of China were gradually forging a new civilization.

It is not known what vehicles these Neolithic peoples of the third millennium B.C. possessed, but legend from a later time relates that the cart was invented by Fu Hsi, one of their fabled rulers. Perhaps this date for the introduction of the wheel into China is not too unreasonable, because it is known that the nomads of Asia were using covered wagons during the same period. The first definite knowledge of the use of wheeled transport comes, however, from the discovery of chariot gear in much later fourteenth-century B.C. burials. No exact reconstruction of these vehicles has been possible, but probably they were similar to the lightly built war chariots discovered in a tomb of the Chou dynasty dated about 300 B.C. Chou chariots had two many-spoked wheels of the sort which have become recognized as typically Chinese. Each chariot was drawn by two horses yoked to a single pole by the inefficient neck harness then in general use throughout the world. No matter how willing the horse, it could not pull its full weight because the harness cut into its throat and choked it. About the beginning of the Christian era the Chinese invented a band which fitted across the horse's shoulders and breast and enabled it to pull much heavier loads than before without discomfort. Shafts, rather than a single pole, were also introduced at about the same time, but although both these important improvements spread quickly in the East, they did not come into general use in Europe until the twelfth century A.D.

The legendary Fu Hsi, of the third millennium B.C. is also supposed to have discovered the raft. Boats of some kind must have been in use long before this, but it may be significant that in the story rafts rather than dugout canoes are mentioned. All the evidence points to Chinese vessels having evolved from the primitive log raft. Canoes can be found nowhere in modern China, while to this day all the traditional craft are without keels and are flat-bottomed. Their whole appearance suggests a built-up raft. Even the name "sampan" for the typical Chinese riverboat means three planks.

8

It is not known when the Chinese first ventured out onto the ocean, but as early as the reign of Emperor Wu, 140–86 B.C., there are records of sea voyages which took five months to complete. Such journeys could only have been undertaken by sailors with a long tradition of seafaring behind them.

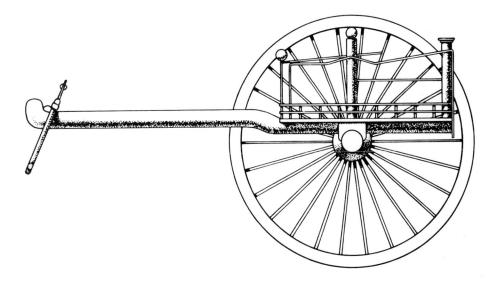

A reconstruction of a Chinese chariot of the 4th century B.C. The multi-spoke wheels were a distinctive feature, but the method of harnessing the horses to a single pole was the same as that used in the Middle East.

Chinese ship designs have altered little over the centuries. Vessels well suited to local conditions were evolved, and the Chinese saw little reason to modify them until they were affected by the impact of modern technology. Pottery models of as far back as the first century A.D. show riverboats remarkably similar to modern sampans. Although traditional designs have survived for so long the Chinese shipbuilders were by no means uninventive.

It is probable that they invented both the rudder and the watertight bulkhead, while during the European Middle Ages their ships were superior to any in the world. Marco Polo, the Venetian traveller of about 1254–1324, noted in amazement their use of four- and even six-masted ships at a time when the largest northern European vessels had to make do with just one. This lead in shipbuilding was not lost until about four hundred years ago.

While the Chinese civilization was still in its infancy, sailors from Egypt and Crete were already braving the sudden squalls of the Mediterranean. Cretan merchants began to trade with neighbouring islands before 3000 B.C., and by 2500 B.C. the island had grown into a powerful nation ruled by the first King Minos. He was succeeded by a long line of kings, all of whom bore the same name; thus, the whole Cretan civilization became known as Minoan. By the time of the first Minos, Cretan ships had begun to make the long journey to Egypt, and as the years rolled by, they became an increasingly common sight on the Nile. Minoan traders were soon known in every important port in the eastern Mediterranean, and their skill as sailors and their cleverness as merchants made Crete into the greatest naval power of her day.

For 1,000 years the Minoans were supreme on the sea and kept their island free from invasion. It was an impressive record, and some credit for it must go to the Cretan shipbuilders. The exact appearance of the Minoan ships is not known, but they were probably more seaworthy than Egyptian boats of the same period. A few distorted pictures do, however, exist on pottery or cut into gemstone seals, and these show ships propelled by both oars and sails. The hulls were flat at one end and curved up at the other, though precisely which end was the bow and which the stern is uncertain. Most authorities claim that it was the bow that curved proudly out of the water, but some think that the flattened part was a ram at the bow, and that it was the stern which was high and curving.

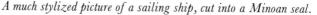

A much stylized picture of a sailing ship, cut into a Minoan seal.

Eventually the Minoan civilization was overwhelmed by invading Greeks from the mainland, who possibly took advantage of the chaos caused by an earthquake on the island. The capital, Knossos, was sacked in about 1400 B.C., and Cretan sea power was destroyed forever.

Another race of seafarers were the Phoenicians. They began their first trading ventures in about 2000 B.C., and when the Minoan Empire fell they easily assumed naval superiority in the Mediterranean. Their earliest ports were on the eastern coast of the Mediterranean, from which they spread out a web of trade routes to the edges of the then-known world. From centres on the Red Sea they reached India and may even have gone as far as China. In the West they sailed out through the Strait of Gibraltar and traded for tin on the western coast of Spain. Tin was vital in those days, because the alloy bronze, made of copper and tin, was the strongest known metal. In their search for tin, the Phoenicians were led still farther north, and traded with what they called the Tin Islands. Once these were thought to be mainland Britain, but now it is believed that they were the Isles of Scilly, off the coast of Cornwall, England. The Phoenicians almost certainly did go to Britain occasionally, but the old legend that they worked mines in Cornwall has no evidence to support it.

The Phoenicians were great sailors and perhaps even greater storytellers. One of the tales that has come down from them still causes argument today. It concerns a sea journey around Africa. If true, it was the most daring voyage of ancient times; if false, it was one of the biggest hoaxes.

The Egyptian Pharaoh, Necho, who reigned in about 600 B.C., wanted to find out whether it was possible to sail around Africa. He hired some Phoenicians, provided them with a fleet of ships, and sent them south out of the Red Sea. For month after month they sailed on, never losing sight of land. The coast of Africa stretched on southward for what must have seemed an eternity, but at last it began to bend, first to the west and then toward the north and home. The Phoenicians claimed that as they sailed west around the tip of Africa the sun was on their right-hand side. This incident made many of the ancients doubt the whole account, because sailors in the Mediterranean always find the sun on their left when they sail westward. Nowadays we can guess that the explorers had crossed the equator, so, of course, the sun would have appeared to change its position.

When the right season came, the Phoenicians landed to plant seeds and waited till the crop had been gathered before pushing on once more. There were probably two such halts, one just after rounding the Cape and another in Morocco. In home waters at last, they must have been happy to pass through the Strait of Gibraltar into their familiar and welcoming Mediterranean and finally back to the Egypt that they had left three long years before. This is the story; if only the Phoenicians had not been such skilled liars, there would be less argument about its truth.

All the main Phoenician cities, Tyre, Sidon, and Acre, were at the eastern end of the Mediterranean. Tyre became the most powerful and founded many colonies that grew into trading cities in their own right. Greatest of these was Carthage, which was established on the north coast of Africa in 800 B.C. The old cities of Phoenicia gradually fell under the sway of the Assyrian Empire and lost much of their importance, but Carthage went from strength to strength on the profits of her trading. She became the undisputed maritime power of the Mediterranean and at the height of her strength had a population of more than 1,000,000.

Like their Phoenician ancestors, the Carthaginians were great explorers. One of their most famous voyages was led by Hanno. In about 425 B.C. he took a fleet of colonists out through the Strait of Gibraltar and sailed along the African coast. Colonies were founded close to the strait; then the expedition crept on along the coast for about 3,000 miles and is believed to have reached Cape Palmas before turning back. The sailors did not enjoy the trip at all. They heard drumbeats and shouts from the shore, while fires reddened the sky at night, so that it seemed that the whole country was being warned of their presence. Probably the sailors' alarm was quite unnecessary, and the flames came from nothing more sinister than seasonal bush fires.

Despite their misgivings, the Carthaginians had to land occasionally for more water. One landing was on an offshore island inhabited by a race of wild and hairy people. Some of the less agile women were cornered so that they might be taken home to Carthage as curiosities. In the course of the journey, however, the wild women proved to be such a nuisance that the sailors finally lost patience and butchered them. The prisoners' unruliness was hardly surprising, because they were almost certainly chimpanzees or gorillas. Eventually the expedition got back to Carthage, and the hairy pelts of the "wild women" were hung in a temple as a thank-offering. This story has been preserved in a Greek version, which claims to be a translation of the leader's own account, and as a result, the modern discoverer of the gorillas gave them their name from the Greek word used to describe Hanno's "wild women."

Clearly, the Phoenicians and Carthaginians must have had fine ships to achieve their remarkable voyages. The Phoenicians had two main types of vessel. One was the "round" ship, used for short trading trips, while the other was the "long" ship, which was used for war or longer journeys.

12

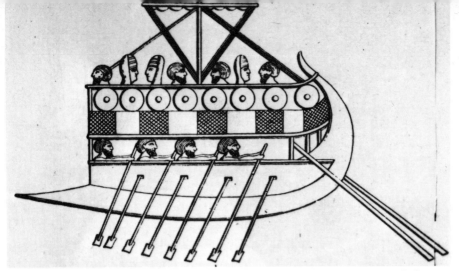

A Phoenician warship armed with a ram. From an Assyrian relief, c. 700 B.C.

A wall relief at Nineveh, dating from about 700 B.C., shows both kinds.

The long ship had two banks of oars and also carried a mast and sail. An upper deck protected the oarsmen from the weather in peacetime and was crowded with warriors bristling with spears and javelins during war. The ship was also armed with a sharply pointed ram in the bow, which was used to hole enemy vessels or break off their oars and render them helpless. Speed and manœuvrability were vital in this sort of naval fighting, so these long ships had long, narrow hulls with a shallow draft. The stern curved up high to give protection from a following wave.

Round ships were smaller in length, but much wider and deeper, so that they could carry more cargo. Bow and stern curved high out of the water, and again there were two banks of oars pulled by oarsmen below deck. The early round ships shown in the Nineveh wall relief carried no sail and relied on oars alone, so they were probably used solely for coastal trade. Both types of ship were steered by long oars trailed in the sea on each side of the stern.

Phoenician boats were strong and seaworthy and, unlike Egyptian vessels, did not need ropes to keep them from breaking up. This was because the tall trees of Phoenicia enabled keels to be made to run the whole length of a ship. Ribs were fixed to this central keel, and planking was attached to the skeleton framework by wooden pegs.

In Phoenician warships the keel stuck out in front of the bow to make the ram. Once it was thought that the Phoenicians had invented this weapon themselves, but now it is usually credited to the people of the Aegean Islands. The wind was too changeable to be relied on for ramming man-œuvres, so sails were lowered, and everything depended on the oarsmen. To increase speed and power, galleys with multiple banks of oars were designed. First came the bireme with two banks of oars, one above the other. Later 13 the trireme with three banks of oars was invented, probably by the Phoenicians of Sidon. Triremes were being built in Egypt during the Pharaoh Necho's reign, so it is quite likely that the expedition he sent out in about 600 B.C. to sail around Africa included some of these craft.

The Phoenicians and Carthaginians were mainly sailors, but when they were compelled to fight on land, their fighting vehicle was the horse-drawn chariot, which was sometimes used in great numbers. At one battle alone, the Carthaginians massed 2,000 two-horse chariots. However, when the Carthaginians discovered a new weapon, the elephant, the popularity of war chariots quickly waned. Elephants were used mainly for their shock effect. They did not carry howdahs, or seats, on their backs in the Indian manner but were driven forward by a man on foot and made to charge into the enemy lines.

A four-horse Grecian war chariot painted on a vase, c. 500 B.C.

2

From 500 B.C. to the Fifteenth Century

The great trading rivals of the Phoenicians in the eastern Mediterranean were the Greeks, while, later, Carthage came into conflict with the expanding Roman Empire and was eventually utterly destroyed. The transport used by the Greeks and Romans was very similar. On land the Greeks had chariots and agricultural wagons. Their chariots had two wheels, usually with four spokes, while the draught animals were attached to a single pole at the front. In both war and racing chariots, the horses were arranged abreast, and sometimes as many as four were used. Years of training were needed to control such teams, and in Greece even rich and famous men thought it no disgrace to compete in chariot races. Farm wagons were much more substantial vehicles, designed to carry heavy loads. They usually had four wheels. Sometimes these were solid disks, but many vase paintings also show farm carts with spoked wheels.

The Romans were the greatest road builders of ancient times. Military roads followed their conquests to the corners of the then-known world, linking armies to their supplies and reinforcements and enabling messengers to speed back to the central power in Rome. In times of peace, trade, as well as military strength, throbbed along these road arteries. At the height of its power the Roman Empire had a road system which extended for 50,000 miles. The Romans themselves did not use chariots for war very often. Instead, they relied on their highly trained infantry and the auxiliary cavalry supplied by subject nations. Chariot racing was, however, one of the favourite spectacles of the Roman mob. Powerful and important men no longer competed, as they had done in Greece, but successful charioteers could still hope for both riches and fame.

But if the Romans neglected wheeled vehicles for war, they did develop them in other ways. A two-wheeled chariot evolved from the British model was used to carry imperial dispatches along the web of long, straight Roman roads. It differed mainly from a war chariot in that it had a seat for the driver, who would be expected to cover many miles in a day. 15

The Romans also adapted the four-wheeled farm wagon and made it into a luxurious vehicle fit to carry people of rank. One improvement which they copied from their Celtic subjects was a front axle that could swivel when turning corners. At first all Roman carts and chariots followed the Greeks, in having a single pole to which the draught animals were harnessed, but later, shafts were used for some purposes. Wall paintings discovered in Pompeii, the town which was buried and preserved by volcanic ash from the eruption of Vesuvius in A.D. 79, show little carts being drawn by goats placed between shafts.

Grecian and Roman galleys were very similar to Phoenician ships from which they probably originated. Although they carried a sail, they relied mainly on oarsmen. Greek-built triremes did not become common until

A model of a Greek trireme, 4th century B.C.

about 500 B.C., but their advantage in speed and power soon made the earlier bireme obsolete. Xenophon, the Greek soldier and writer, tells of a trireme which kept up a speed of 9 mph for more than a day. During the fourth century B.C. galleys with four and five banks of oars were invented, probably by the ingenious Greeks. One ancient writer attributed them to a particular man. Dionysius, who was tyrant of the Greek city of Syracuse in Sicily.

16

A Greek merchantship under sail. From a vase, c. 500 B.C.

The Romans were not natural sailors, as were the Greeks, but they reluctantly took to the water to attack Carthage on her own element, the sea. The Romans, lacking experience as seafarers, realized that the usual ramming tactics would favour the Carthaginians, who were famous for their skill in handling ships. What the Romans needed was a secret weapon to take the Carthaginians completely by surprise.

When the opposing fleets met at Mylae in 260 B.C., the Carthaginians closed in, expecting an easy victory. Full of confidence, they rowed straight for the Roman ships, trying to ram them or shatter their oars. When they came within range, however, the Romans suddenly revealed their carefully kept secret. Each of their galleys had a sort of drawbridge slung to its mast. These were let down with a rush onto the Carthaginians' ships, and immediately, heavily armed Roman soldiers swarmed across onto their opponents' decks. Bewildered by this new tactic, the Carthaginian fleet re-formed and tried again, but every onslaught was resisted. In the end their fleet broke in disorder, and the Romans either captured or sank fifty of their enemy's galleys. It was a blow from which the sea power of Carthage never recovered.

Galleys had such large crews of oarsmen that there was little space left for cargo. The Greeks, like other Mediterranean peoples, had a much wider and deeper ship, which they used for trading. Vase paintings of these round ships show that they were propelled mainly by sail.

The Romans also had this type of merchantman, which they eventually developed into the best sailing ship of the ancient world. Their greatest

17

single improvement was the introduction, at the beginning of the Christian Era, of a second mast, or artemon, which was angled forward to project over the bow. The sail carried on the new mast allowed ships to balance better on the breeze, and for the first time in antiquity, large sailing vessels were able to make real progress against an adverse wind.

Another Roman innovation was the use of two small triangular sails fitted above the yardarm of the mainmast to give valuable extra sail area in very calm weather. With all these improvements, the Roman merchant

This relief of about A.D. 200 shows Roman two-masted merchant ships. The second mast, or artemon, was angled forwards over the bow.

ship became almost independent of oars except for manœuvring in harbour. At sea, oars were seldom used unless the vessel was becalmed.

The grain carriers which plied between the North African granaries and Italy were typical Roman merchantmen. Often they reached lengths of as much as 95 feet and could carry loads of some 250 tons. Like most other

Roman vessels, they were guided by two steering oars, placed one on each side of the ship.

When Roman power crumbled as a result of barbarian invasions and internal decadence in the fourth and fifth centuries A.D., Western Europe suffered a great setback. A depleted Roman Empire survived in the East, but there was no longer one government administering the area covered by most of modern Europe, Asia Minor, and North Africa. As a result, there was not the same need to maintain high standards of communications. The efficient sailing ship with its artemon vanished, and in the West, roads were allowed to decay through neglect, and chaos ruled.

Before considering the sombre period which followed the decline of the Roman Empire, there is a more entertaining topic which deserves mention — the early history of flight.

Of course, men in ancient times could not fly, but the thought of flying provided a constant source of daydreams and stories. People watched the birds and envied them the freedom of the air. But if men themselves had to stay earthbound, they could at least give their gods the power of flight. In nearly every culture, bulls, horses, lions, or whatever else served as divinities were given wings.

The legend of Daedalus and Icarus. This woodcut, dating from 1493, was the first picture of human flight to appear in a printed book.

There were even some legends about ordinary men who took to the air. Perhaps the most famous of these mythical airmen were Daedalus and his son, Icarus, who were unjustly imprisoned by the cruel King Minos of Crete. The story tells how Daedalus made wings from wax and feathers so that they could leap from a window and escape. When all was ready, the father solemnly warned the boy not to fly too close to the sun lest the wax melt. Unfortunately, Icarus was so pleased with his newly found power that he   19 forgot his father's advice and soared higher and higher, without noticing that the wax was softening. One after another, the feathers fell from the wax until the wings became useless, and Icarus fell to his death in the sea near the island of Ikaria, which still bears his name.

Icarus's legendary fall must have been the first aeronautical casualty, unless precedence is given to King Bladud, an equally legendary ruler of Britain. Bladud is famed chiefly as the father of the King Lear of Shakespeare's play and for his powers of sorcery. Occasionally he tried to fly, but one day he must have muddled his spells, for in 852 B.C. he was killed while attempting a flight.

Another tale is about the Persian Emperor Kai Kawus, who combined a desire to fly with the strong belief that exercise was unbecoming to a person of his exalted rank. There was to be no undignified flapping of wings for him. Something else could do the work. So four hungry eagles were fettered to the corners of his throne, with juicy pieces of meat suspended above them. According to the story, the eagles lifted the monarch but then tired and let Kai Kawus down with such a painful bump that he was cured of any further wish to fly.

A Persian painting of the Emperor Kai Kawus on his eagle-powered throne.

Archaeological discoveries are the main source of information about European transport during the fifth to tenth centuries. One of the greatest finds was made in 1939 at Sutton Hoo in Suffolk, where the remains of a large Saxon rowing boat were unearthed. Unfortunately, all the timbers had rotted, but a clear imprint was left in the sandy soil where the vessel had lain for centuries, so that a mental picture of the ship could be built up and drawings made. It was an open rowing boat about eighty feet long and fourteen feet across at its widest. There was no mast to carry a sail, so it must have relied completely on its oarsmen. A keel, from which ribs fanned out, ran the whole length of the boat and made it strong and sea-worthy. The archaeologists believe the ship to date from about A.D. 650 but to be of a type similar to that used about 200 years before, during the early Saxon invasions of England.

In Scandinavia archaeologists have been lucky enough to dig up almost complete boats. One of these was the ancient ship found preserved in a bog

After 1,200 years in the ground, the timbers of the Sutton Hoo boat had rotted away but had left a clear imprint in the soil.

in Nydam, Denmark. It is thought to have been built during the fourth century A.D., and like the later Sutton Hoo ship, it was an open rowing boat with no mast or sail. Probably it was a war boat used to carry raiding parties during the summer months, for with its length of 73 feet, its narrow beam, and its lack of a genuine keel it could never have withstood winter storms on the open sea.

Because both these early ships lacked masts, it is sometimes thought that sails were unknown in northern Europe during the first few centuries of the 21

Christian Era. Archaeological discoveries, however, do not give the whole picture. There is also the evidence of written history. The Romans tell how the Veneti, a Celtic people who lived on the Atlantic coast of what is now France, made great use of the wind. In fact, they were so skilful with their animal hide sails in pre-Christian times that they very nearly defeated a Roman fleet under the command of the famous Julius Caesar. The Romans managed to save the day only by cutting through their opponents' rigging with knives mounted on long poles. There are also records of the sixth-century monks of Iona using sail-driven ships, while in A.D. 470 a Bishop of Clermont wrote of Saxons returning home under swelling sails.

But although sails were in use, there were certainly parts of northern Europe where sailing ships were a rarity, since in A.D. 560 the Byzantine author Procopius wrote of the English as barbarians who did not use the sail but relied on oars. In all probability, sails were not widely adopted in England and Scandinavia until the sixth century, but after that date they were developed very rapidly.

The finest ships in Europe during these centuries were built by the Vikings, or inlet men, as their name means. These Vikings began to raid the shores of northern Europe in the latter part of the eighth century A.D., spreading terror and destruction in their wake. Armed bands would descend unexpectedly on remote houses and villages. At first it was mainly isolated monasteries that suffered, but, later, whole coastlines were harried. Much of the Vikings' success was due to their superb ships, which took them on some amazing voyages. Fortunately, a number of their vessels have been recovered almost intact from burial mounds, so that the method of construction is known exactly.

The best preserved of these buried ships was dug out of a mound in Gokstad, Norway, in 1880. It dates from about A.D. 900 and was a vast improvement on the much earlier Nydam ship. The Gokstad vessel is built of solid oak throughout and has a strongly made single-piece keel. Its stem and stern curve up high, but amidships it lay low in the water. Overall it measures seventy-nine feet in length, while it is nearly seventeen feet wide. Ribs increase the strength of the boat. Surprisingly, the lower planks were tied to these ribs and not fixed in place with iron spikes, as were the planks above the waterline. This was to make the boat more elastic so that it could stand up to really rough weather on the open sea. The planking was put on in clinker fashion, each plank overlapping the one immediately below it, and the gaps were caulked with tarred rope. When the ship was discovered, the mast was not complete, but experts have worked out that it must have been about forty feet high. It fitted into a very heavy oak block

This graceful Viking ship was buried at Gokstad in about A.D. 900. It was discovered and dug from its mound in 1880.

amidships and carried a square sail. There was also provision for sixteen pairs of oars, which were worked through holes in the sides of the ship. When the boat was running before the wind on its sail alone, the holes could be closed to stop water from slopping through.

In harbour it was a Viking custom for the warriors to hang their shields along the sides of their ships. They loved colour and display and would often

23

paint the shields alternately yellow and black to give a decorative effect. The Gokstad ship had room for thirty-three overlapping shields on each side, so it must have carried quite a large crew. The helmsman stood in the stern and guided the boat with a single steering oar that was fitted to the starboard or steerboard side. A horizontal tiller stuck out from the top of the steering oar shaft so that the oar could be turned easily.

The Vikings expressed their taste for bright, gaudy colours in their choice of sails. Ancient drawings cut into rocks show Viking ships with chequered sails, while Old Norse stories tell of white sails with red or blue stripes. On a sunlit sea, a Viking fleet must have been a stirring sight.

When another burial ship was excavated in Oseberg, Norway, a cart and several sleds were found among the buried possessions, so something is also known about the land transport used by the Vikings in the ninth century. The sledges were probably peculiar to Scandinavia, but almost certainly the cart was similar to those in use throughout northern Europe at this time. It had four wheels, which were spoked but had extremely thick rims. The bodywork was mounted on a central rib and was highly ornate. Magnificent carvings covered the sides of the cart in a profusion

The ornate Oseberg cart, a ceremonial vehicle from the Viking era.

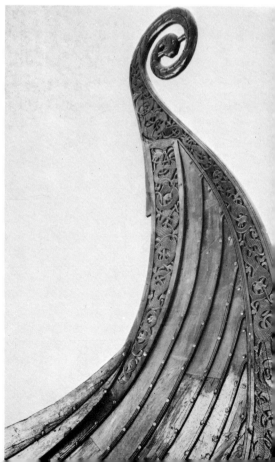

The beautiful curving prow of the Oseberg ship.

which suggests that this was a special vehicle reserved for ceremonial duties. However, in the same burial mound a few scraps of tapestry were found, which showed both open and covered four-wheeled wagons. These indicate that carts were far more common in Scandinavia than might have been expected from the almost complete lack of roads. Probably they came mainly from the lowland areas, where they could have been used as farm wagons.

All the sledges that were found with the boat, except one which was obviously intended for everyday use, were highly ornate. During the frozen northern winters the Vikings preferred to travel overland, instead of by sea, and must have used their man-drawn sledges very extensively. However, they also had another way of travelling over snow, because even then the Scandinavians were experts on skis.

During their summer sailing season they made some amazing journeys into the North Atlantic in their open long ships. Vikings colonized Iceland in the ninth century and from there discovered and settled Greenland during the latter part of the tenth century. Even then their restless spirit drove them on. The Old Norse sagas tell how, five centuries before Columbus, they set foot on the shores of America. They were too far from home to found a permanent colony in what they called Vinland, probably modern New England, but one can only wonder at the endurance and courage of a race of men who could find their way across the wide Atlantic Ocean in open boats.

However, the Vikings were not the only ones to make great voyages. In the Middle East, the teachings of Mohammed had given a sense of unity and purpose to the Arab people and filled them with a great upsurge of energy, which for a time put them in advance of the Europeans. The Prophet died in A.D. 632, and within 20 years the Arabs had conquered most of western Asia and North Africa. Later they overran Spain, gained a foothold in Sicily, and even penetrated into France. Eventually their warlike ardour cooled, and they established a civilization which was much more progressive than European society of the same period.

One of the ways in which Arab superiority showed itself was in the fine design of their ships and the daring of their merchant venturers. During the ninth century A.D. Arab ships reached India and China, and one trader, Suleiman, is mentioned by name as having made several journeys to these countries.

Arab vessels used a kind of rigging that had developed in the eastern Mediterranean at the beginning of the Christian Era. It consisted of a triangular sail set on a yardarm which ran fore and aft and which sloped 25 down almost to the deck. The lateen, as it was called, could make use of wind coming from either side of the ship and was quite an advance on single square sails, which were more suited to a following breeze. Arab conquests had by the ninth century spread the use of the more efficient lateen sails over the whole Mediterranean, but despite the change in rigging, hulls showed little alteration and were almost identical to those on Roman ships of 700 years earlier. Twin steering oars, one set on each quarter, and carvel construction were used exactly as in earlier times. Carvel-built boats have their planking butted together edge to edge, as opposed to clinker building, where the planks overlap. The Arabs also revived the Roman idea of using two masts. Fitted with lateen sails, these two-masted ships sailed very well and once again became common in the Mediterranean.

An aeronautical story comes from the same period. A Shah of Persia, who lived in the tenth century, had a beautiful tower built for himself. When it was finished, the Shah was delighted but rewarded the architect by imprisoning him on the roof of his own creation so that no one else could use his skill to build a rival tower. Nothing could move the unjust Shah, and at last the luckless architect hit on a desperate scheme to escape. He claimed that vultures were attacking him and asked for wood to build a little hut for protection. Reluctantly the Shah agreed, and the prisoner set to work—not on a shelter, but on a pair of wings. When these were finished, he strapped them on and glided safely down to freedom. This is a good illustration of man's abiding interest in flight, although, of course, it has no more truth than the legend of Daedalus.

Meanwhile, Europe was gradually settling down. By the tenth and eleventh centuries an ordered society based on the feudal ownership of land was replacing the former chaos. At the head of the feudal community was the king, who owned most of the land. Important nobles held great tracts of territory directly from him, while lesser men might have several overlords between themselves and the king. All held their land on condition that they rendered service and obedience to the person immediately above them. This encouraged a static society where everyone knew his place, and most men kept to it. It was not an age calculated to encourage invention and originality.

The type of ship perfected by the Vikings remained predominant in northern Europe well into feudal times. This is amply illustrated in the famous Bayeux tapestry, which chronicles the Norman invasion of England in 1066 and shows both Norman and Saxon vessels, neither of which differ significantly from their Norse ancestors. During the twelfth century European ships began at last to change from the Viking pattern, mainly

The Norman and Saxon ships embroidered on the Bayeux Tapestry differed little from Viking vessels.

because of an increase in trade. Open galleys with large crews of oarsmen had little room left for cargo, so a new type of ship was needed. Greater reliance was put on sails, crews were reduced, and vessels were widened and deepened so that they could carry more. The graceful Viking lines slowly disappeared, and northern boats took on a stumpy look. Despite these changes, one traditional feature remained—ships were still steered by a single oar fastened to the starboard side.

The Crusades also gave rise to changes in design. When the first Crusaders reached the Middle East at the very end of the eleventh century, they found an Arab civilization far in advance of their own; Arabs seemed to live in luxury and to be full of new ideas. Even their ships were different. Two or three masts were quite common in the Mediterranean, although no northern European ship had more than one sail at that time. Most Arab ships also carried temporary fighting towers, which could be put up just before a battle. From these vantage points, stones and arrows could be showered onto the enemy decks below. The fighting towers must have given the Crusaders both a shock and an inspiration, for subsequently, during the twelfth century, European ships began to carry towers, too. Usually there was one in the bow and one in the stern, while a small platform, or fighting top was often built near the head of the mast. As far as is known, the other Arab idea of twin masts was not copied until much later.

During the thirteenth century many seaports used town seals which had pictures of ships on them. The seal of Sandwich, dating from 1238, shows a typical ship of the period. It was a squat, dumpy vessel with a single mast and high, upward-curving bow and stern. Fore- and aftercastles appeared to have been temporarily added, and a bowsprit stuck out over the bow. This little mast carried no sail but, instead, served as a fixing point for ropes and a support for a small grapnel, or anchor.

As the thirteenth century progressed, the fighting towers became permanent features and ceased to look as if they had been stuck on as a hasty afterthought. Steering oars still remained common, but towards the end of the previous century some European ships had begun to use rudders hung from their sternposts. This more efficient method of steering seems to have originated in Han China and to have taken a thousand years to spread   27 across the world to the West. The seal of Ipswich of A.D. 1200 bears the earliest known picture of a European ship equipped with a rudder.

The adoption of the rudder caused a considerable change in hull design. Sternposts were made straighter so that rudders could be fitted more easily, and for the first time in history the bows and sterns of northern European ships could easily be told apart.

At the same time, forecastles were also changing in appearance. They kept their old function as fighting towers, but their square shape was gradually moulded into a triangle so that they fitted better into the pointed bow. The after- or summercastle kept its square shape but was enlarged to make covered accommodation for important passengers.

European ships had not altered much more by the fourteenth century. They were still single-masted and somewhat dumpy, but those owned by noblemen had sails decorated with heraldic badges. Some of the gold coins of Edward III's reign carry a picture of one of his ships, and it is said that they were struck to commemorate the great naval Battle of Sluys in 1340, when a force of English ships under the king's personal command destroyed a whole French fleet.

Land transport in feudal Europe was characterized by terrible roads. In winter they became rivers of mud, while in summer they were deeply rutted and covered with dust. Light goods were carried by packhorses with panniers, or baskets suspended on either side, but for heavier loads, carts were used in surprising numbers. Medieval pictures show that the carts often had treads on their wheels, and these must have been needed frequently to give purchase on the treacherous roads. Fortunately, the methods of harnessing long used in the Far East spread into Europe during the twelfth and thirteenth centuries. Padded horse collars and shafts replaced the single pole and neck harness. Horses were able to pull up to five times more powerfully than before, but in spite of this speeds were still very low. Even when a convoy of carts was rushing a Scottish king's ransom south into England in 1375, the drivers could coax only thirty-six miles a day out of their straining teams.

Passenger travel had declined, and it was thought unmanly to ride in any sort of vehicle. The only way for a gentleman to travel was on horseback, and even much humbler people rode in the saddle if their pockets allowed. It was only the sick or women of noble birth who enjoyed the doubtful luxury of the horse-drawn litter. The litter was a sort of couch mounted on two poles. The ends of each pole were harnessed to horses, and if the animals moved at anything more than a walk, the passenger must have been tossed around most uncomfortably.

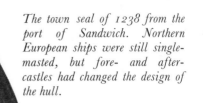

The town seal of 1238 from the port of Sandwich. Northern European ships were still single-masted, but fore- and after-castles had changed the design of the hull.

The first-known picture of a European rudder-steered ship appears on the seal of the town of Ipswich dated A.D. 1200.

Like all other times, the Middle Ages had its share of dreamers and men of vision. Some had their imagination stirred by the effortless example of the birds and longed to conquer the air. Enthusiasts reasoned that if man made wings that were big and strong enough, then he, too, would be able to flap himself into the air.

In the eleventh century men began to put their dreams into action, and the suicidal sport of tower jumping became almost fashionable. Daring but foolhardy men plummeted to their doom from high towers, flapping their pitifully inadequate wings. One of the earliest was a Saracen, who decided to demonstrate his aeronautical art before a really distinguished audience. As it happened, the Byzantine emperor and the Turkish sultan were attending games at the hippodrome in Constantinople, and they seemed suitably eminent. The Saracen put on a cloak with rigid stiffeners and threw himself from a tower into the arena, thinking that he would glide down in safety. He survived the actual fall but broke so many bones that he died shortly afterward. Some tower-jumpers were more fortunate and escaped with their lives, but none made any progress toward achieving flight.

Even a really great man, Roger Bacon, the English friar and scientist, who lived from about 1214 to 1294 made no real advance, although he speculated and wrote about man-carrying flying machines. Bacon was a prophet who could see what lay in the future, rather than an actual inventor.

Opposite: *The horse-drawn litter in this medieval painting carried Isabella of France on the way to her betrothal to Richard II of England in 1396.*

31

Canterbury Pilgrims leaving Canterbury: 'The only way for a gentleman to travel was on horseback, and even much humbler people rode in the saddle if their pockets allowed.'

3

The Fifteenth Century

The fifteenth century was a century of change. Europe was aroused from the torpor of the Middle Ages. Men began to ask questions and to look for answers in their own experiences rather than in ancient books. There was a new interest in both the arts and the sciences. This was the Age of the Renaissance.

Even ships changed remarkably. In 1400 the typical European ship had only one mast and sail and needed a following breeze to achieve any speed. By the end of the century three-masters with much better sailing characteristics were common. It was probably improved ship design, more than any other factor, which made the century famous for its great voyages of exploration.

For centuries the people of Europe had known that the Arabs used two- and three-masted ships, but they had been slow to follow this example, because their own vessels were small enough to manage reasonably well on one sail. By the early fifteenth century this situation was beginning to change. Thousand-tonners were not unknown, and the need for more sails was becoming urgent.

Two-masted ships came first. Henry V's giant *Grace à Dieu* of 1418 had a second mast, and a fifteenth-century painting in Canterbury Cathedral shows two twin-masted boats, both with typical European square sails.

Three-masters followed quickly and were probably in use several decades before their earliest known picture appeared on a seal of 1466. At first there was only one sail to each mast. The central mainmast had a large square sail, while the aftermast, or mizzen, supported a triangular lateen sail mounted fore-and-aft in the Arab fashion. The forward mast carried a tiny square sail, which was of little value for propulsion.

Initially, the forward mast was placed very near the bow, where its sail could best stop the ship from swinging around into a wind from the beam. Toward the end of the century this function was taken over by a spritsail attached to the bowsprit, which stuck out over the bow. The forward mast

33

This 15th-century fresco from Canterbury Cathedral, which illustrates the legend of St Eustace, includes two twin-masted boats with typical European square sails.

was then moved farther back to where the deck was much wider. Here the mast was secured far more firmly, because the supporting ropes which ran from its head to the sides of the ship could be anchored much farther apart than before. A bigger sail could now be carried without endangering the mast in stormy weather, and for the first time the foresail made a real contribution to the driving power of the ship.

This was not the only improvement. A small topsail was added above the mainsail, and before the century ended, even the forward mast was fitted with a second sail. The spread of canvas was increased in yet another way, for in the late years of the fifteenth century a fourth mast was introduced. Henry VII's *Regent* of 1487 was the first English four-master.

It was also during the fifteenth century that specially designed warships made their appearance. Until then it had always been the custom to use the same ships in war and peace. The king simply hired boats from the merchants whenever he needed a fleet. Cannon eventually altered all this. When they were first installed on ships in the middle of the fourteenth

A model of an English three-masted ship of the late 15th century. As yet, each mast carries only one sail.

century, the cannon were still small enough to be mounted comfortably on the aftercastles of ordinary merchantmen. A hundred years later, cannon had grown so much in size and power that they had to be installed down on the main deck so that the ship would not get too top-heavy. Even the smaller cannon were moved to lower positions inside the fore- and aftercastles and fired through specially cut portholes. Kings were forced to commission large vessels specially built as warships, and national navies began to form. This was a slow business. Even in Elizabeth I's time the royal fleet was of no great size, so that merchantmen were still often hired.

As European ships increased in size, the old method of clinker building gradually fell into disfavour, and large boats were constructed in the carvel 35 fashion. Planks no longer overlapped but instead were butted together edge to edge in the Mediterranean manner to guarantee the really strong structure needed for big ships.

As the ships of the fifteenth century improved, the voyages of exploration grew more daring. The Portuguese worked their way steadily down the coast of Africa, and in 1488 one of their captains, Bartholomew Diaz, became the first European to round the Cape of Good Hope—the most southerly point of Africa. According to tradition, the explorer chose the name Cape of Storms, but this was altered by the Portuguese king to its present optimistic title. Unfortunately, Diaz's choice of a name proved all too accurate, and in a later voyage he was drowned in a shipwreck off that very cape.

Even before Diaz made his ill-fated voyage, another Portuguese, Vasco Da Gama, had won the race to India. He sailed from Lisbon in 1497 with a fleet of four vessels, and followed Diaz's route to the Cape of Good Hope. Despite bad weather, this was rounded without mishap, and the expedition sailed on up the east coast of Africa until they were lucky enough to find a pilot who knew the way to India. On his advice they struck out eastward across an open and unknown sea. After twenty-three tense days the blue blur of the Indian coast came in sight. The expedition was safe, and at last, after nearly a year of voyaging, a sea-route to the fabulous East had been found.

But not all the explorers were Portuguese. Columbus, the most famous of them all, came from Genoa in Italy. Like the other adventurers of his day, Columbus wanted to find a way to the wealth of the Indies, but he had a new idea of how to get there. As an educated man, he realized that the earth was a sphere and so understood that India could be reached by journeying either to the east or to the west. He chose to try the western route and began to search for someone to finance an expedition. Columbus was turned down by nearly every court in Europe, but at last he secured the favour of Queen Isabella of Castile. She supplied him with three ships, the *Santa María* of 100 tons, the *Pinta* of 50 tons, and the *Niña* of 40 tons, which were small even by the standards of those days.

In 1492 the little fleet left Spain and made for the Canary Islands, where fresh supplies were taken on board. Then Columbus led his ships to the west, into an ocean where none had dared to sail before. Every day took them farther into the unknown, and eventually the sailors began to lose their nerve and murmur against their captain. Mutiny was in the air, but just in time, land was sighted and confidence restored. The first landfall was on Watling Island in the Bahamas and later the explorers visited Cuba and Hispaniola. Columbus had found his way to the outlying islands of the New World, but he did not realize what he had discovered. Until the day

36

Ships of Vasco da Gama's fleet.

A full-size replica of Columbus' Santa María *made for the New York World's Fair of 1964–65.*

he died, he still believed that the lands he had reached were parts of the Indies. Even the present name for the islands, West Indies, enshrines this belief.

While all these great things were happening at sea, land transport plodded on much as it had done for years. There were no striking innovations during the fifteenth century.

With flight, the story was different. Tower jumping started again, but, of course, met with no more success than before. The Italian mathematician Danti was one of those who tried to fly. In about 1490 he made a pair of rigid gliding wings and jumped from a high tower in his native city of Perugia. The glide went well until one of the wings collapsed under the strain. Danti survived the crash, and there is even a story that he was brave enough to attempt another flight.

Leonardo da Vinci (1452–1519) was another and far greater Italian.

A design for a helicopter found in Leonardo da Vinci's notebooks.

Both artist and scientist, he combined rich powers of imagination with great experimental skill. The problems of flight caught and held his attention, and his fertile brain produced many designs for flying machines.

Leonardo worked out two completely original aeronautical inventions—the parachute and the helicopter. Both of these were illustrated and described in his famous notebooks. The picture of the parachute showed a man floating downward, suspended from a sort of pyramid-shaped tent, while a nearby entry commented on air resistance. Leonardo's helicopter was even more remarkable. It had a rotor that looked like a flattened corkscrew, which was supposed to twist and screw the machine into the air. Entries in the notebooks suggest that Leonardo may even have built a model of his helicopter and flown it successfully.

The great Italian also studied the way in which birds fly and designed man-carrying ornithopters to imitate their flapping flight. He drew several ingenious contraptions with levers that allowed the pilot to waggle the wings up and down. No one knows whether any machines were built to these plans. It is to be hoped not, for despite Leonardo's cleverness, they could never have worked and would have been a disappointment to him.

Leonardo da Vinci pointed the way to the future. He was an engineer with great powers of imagination. Unfortunately, his notes were lost for centuries and lay forgotten and unread until 1797. By then the rest of the world had caught up, and men had already learned to fly in balloons. Leonardo's writings could teach little, but they were still a splendid example for other pioneers.

39

Henry VIII's fleet at Dover in 1520. Several of the larger vessels have four masts, and topsails have been added above the mainsails.

4

The Sixteenth and Seventeenth Centuries

The sixteenth century more than made up for any lack of progress in land transport during the previous hundred years, for improvements and innovations followed one another rapidly. Most important in the long run were the primitive railways which appeared in some German coal mines during the first half of the century. They were introduced to ease the job of guiding heavily laden trucks along narrow, twisting passageways. At first the wagons were kept on course by metal pins which jutted down from beneath them and ran along a groove between the closely spaced rails. Later in the century someone had the better idea of fitting flanges to the insides of the wheels to prevent them from jumping the track. The distance between rails was then increased to give the wagons a much wider wheel base so that they would not tip over so easily when rounding a corner. English collieries lagged behind, and it was 1597 before a railway was installed in one. Despite this lack of early enthusiasm, it was in Britain that railways were eventually developed into a new method of passenger travel which altered the whole world.

A 16th-century German mine wagon with flanged wheels—an ancestor of modern rolling stock.

The German miners were not by any means the first people to use railways. The idea goes much further back in history. Greece was one of the ancient countries to use rails of a sort. Even some of the Greek roads were more like railways than anything else and consisted of two specially prepared ruts. Carts and wagons ran along these grooves, just as our trains run on tracks. An even closer approach to a modern railway was the set of wooden rails which spanned the narrow Isthmus of Corinth. Ships were beached and hauled over this track so that a long sea journey around the Peloponnese could be avoided. However, the sixteenth-century miners of Germany were probably ignorant of this previous use of rails and deserve full credit for inventiveness.

Road transport in sixteenth-century Europe was undergoing some changes. Passenger-carrying wagons were greatly improved by the suspension of their bodywork on leather straps, which meant a far less bumpy ride for the inmates. These new vehicles became known as coaches, probably from the Hungarian village of Kocs, where they are supposed to have been first made. Coaches also had pivoted front wheels, which allowed corners to be turned far more easily. This idea went back to Roman times but had been forgotten for many years until it was rediscovered in the fifteenth century, when carriages carrying heavy siege guns had to be manœuvred.

The coach was introduced into England by a Dutchman, who later

*Coaches belonging to Queen Elizabeth I of England on their way to her palace of Nonsuch.
Late 16th century.*

became coachman to Elizabeth I. Her coach, like all the early ones, had to contend with such rough and muddy roads that the driver could not manage without the aid of postilions who rode the horses and helped urge them forward when the going got particularly bad.

Road conditions did not improve very much during the next hundred years, and in the seventeenth century, laws had to be passed to stop them from getting even worse. One of these laws compelled owners of heavy wagons to fit them with iron tyres at least four inches wide, so that their wheels did not sink into the road and leave deep, dangerous ruts. Another law even banished the fairly light passenger-carrying stage wagons from the highways for a time.

Meanwhile, the design of coaches improved steadily. In about 1665 steel springs replaced leather straps, and in 1669 Samuel Pepys mentioned in his diary that his carriage had glass windows—luxury indeed!

Changes in ship design during the sixteenth and seventeenth centuries were slow but sure. More and larger sails were carried, while hulls had to be strengthened and modified as cannon became bigger and heavier. By the late 1400's deck-mounted guns had grown so weighty that warships were becoming dangerously top-heavy. A way out of this difficulty was devised by the Frenchman Decharges, who thought of mounting the cannon below deck and firing them through holes cut in the hull itself. The practise spread quickly through the European navies, and by 1514 it was general in the English fleet. Gradually these gunports extended in a continuous line along the entire length of the ship to give a bristling broadside of cannon. Before long, even this formidable armament was not enough, and larger warships, like the *Harry Grace à Dieu*, which was rebuilt in 1540, were given a second row of guns mounted on a still lower deck.

The *Harry Grace à Dieu* was the most famous English ship of her day. She was originally launched in 1514 and was a four-masted thousand-tonner. Her four masts carried a considerable spread of canvas. The forward and mainmast each sported three square sails—mainsails at the bottom, above them topsails, and, highest of all, the tiny topgallants. The next mast was called the main mizzen, and the fourth one was known as the bonaventure mizzen. Both had triangular fore-and-aft mainsails, but in addition, they were equipped with lateen-type topsails, while the main mizzen even had a triangular topgallant. Lateen topsails, however, proved so difficult to handle that they were used only on very big ships and soon went out of service altogether. When mizzen topsails were successfully reintroduced early in the seventeenth century, the upper lateen was replaced by a much more manageable square sail.

43

The four-masted Harry Grace à Dieu *painted by Anthony Anthony in 1546.*

The sixteenth century, like the fifteenth, was a time of great voyages, and greatest of all was the first circumnavigation of the globe. This was started in 1519, when Ferdinand Magellan, a Portuguese in the service of Spain, led a fleet of five vessels out into the Atlantic and headed for South America. By October, 1520, the expedition had reached the southerly tip of the New World and, for the first time, ran into serious difficulties. The route lay through the twisting and dangerous channel which is now called the Strait of Magellan, and the passage lasted for thirty-eight nerve-racking days. At last the little armada won its way into open water again, but not before one ship had deserted and the rest had come near to turning back.

After this, the new ocean they entered seemed friendly and welcoming. Gentle winds wafted the fleet across its wide expanse, and the delighted Magellan named it the Pacific. However, though its winds seemed kind, the

44

very size of the ocean made it hostile to puny humans. For ninety-eight days the fleet sailed on and in that time found only two desert islands. Scurvy broke out among the crew because of lack of fresh vegetables, and provisions of all sorts ran so low that oxhides and sawdust were eaten, and even rats became delicacies.

Eventually, in March, 1521, the exhausted expedition reached the group of islands which Magellan named the Ladrones from the Spanish word for thief—a reflection of his view of the islanders. Here the fleet was restocked, and the famished men refreshed themselves for a little while before the ships sailed again. This time they were only at sea a few days before they came to another group of islands—the Philippines. During the exploration of this archipelago Magellan was killed in a battle with the Filipinos, and the rest of the expedition became so depleted that one of the remaining ships had to be burned, because there were insufficient men to crew her.

The sad remnants of the expedition found their way to Borneo and then on to the Moluccas, which they reached in November, 1521. Here it was found that only one ship, the *Vittoria*, was seaworthy enough to continue, so part of the expedition had to be left behind when the lone ship set out for Europe. The journey home very nearly proved disastrous. Heavy seas and adverse winds delayed her progress, and again deadly scurvy followed in the wake of starvation. By the time the Cape of Good Hope was rounded, many of the men were sick or dying. Their condition had become so bad that they decided to land in the Cape Verde Islands for provisions, but even this proved unfortunate, for the Portuguese authorities seized and imprisoned part of the crew. Finally, the *Vittoria* won through, but at great cost, for when she sailed into Seville Harbour in 1522 to become the first ship to sail around the world, there were only 19 sailors on board, the survivors of an expedition of about 280 men.

Perhaps as a result of the experience gained in these long expeditions, ship design showed definite improvements during the latter part of the sixteenth century. Ships grew slimmer, and the contours below the waterline were altered so that vessels could slide through the water more easily. Changes in rigging, like the innovation of the square mizzen topsail that was tried out at the beginning of the seventeenth century were generally the results of good guesses and experiments. The success of the mizzen topsail quickly spelled the doom of four-masted ships. It was soon realized that a single large mizzen mast with the new rigging was far more effective than two smaller ones. By 1640 the English fleet contained no four-masters at all.

The fore- and mainmasts had long since ceased being single poles. They had a very stout lower part, to the top of which was lashed a thinner topmast. 45

On very big ships there was even a third part, called the topgallant mast. A particularly important innovation of the late sixteenth century was the development of a method by which the upper masts could be detached and lowered to the deck if bad weather threatened. This encouraged the use of tall masts, which were able to carry still more sails.

One of the earliest ships really to exploit tall masts was the *Sovereign of the Seas*, which was built in 1637. Each of her two foremasts carried four sails

Magellan's death in the Philippines taken from a contemporary drawing. The Vittoria *or* Victoria *later completed her voyage to become the first ship to sail around the world.*

—a mainsail, topsail, topgallant, and, above them all, a tiny royal. The mizzenmast had two square sails above its triangular lateen. However, the *Sovereign of the Seas* was a freak ship that had come before its time. Royals did not come into general use until another century and a half had elapsed.

Although much was happening on land and sea during the sixteenth century, would-be aviators were scarce. Men were so busy exploring the surface of the earth that few seemed to have spared a thought for the sky. One who did was a glib Italian called John Damian. In 1501 he arrived in Edinburgh and quickly established himself as a favourite in the court of James IV of Scotland. Damian's tongue usually got him exactly what he wanted, but on one famous occasion in 1507 he went too far. His boastful claims of knowing the secret of flight were taken up, and he was challenged to fly from the battlements of Stirling Castle. Damian was naturally somewhat disconcerted, but too proud to back down. There was nothing for it but to make a pair of feathered wings and hope for the best. Thus equipped, the unwilling birdman mounted to the battlements and jumped. He plummeted, rather than flew, and ended up half-buried in a dung heap, which added to the ignominy but saved him from anything worse than a broken leg. Most men would have been silenced by the sheer indignity of the mishap, but Damian was still able to come out with a plausible excuse. His mistake, he claimed, had been in choosing hens' and not eagles' feathers for his wings. Naturally, such wings as these had preferred the farmyard to the higher airs. No doubt his listeners were impressed by his quick wit, but they must have noticed that the clever Italian never put the eagles' feathers to a practical test.

Much more important was the seventeenth-century plan for an aerial ship, which was included in a book published by the scientist Father Francesco de Lana in 1670. This design is rightly famous, because it is the first properly thought-out scheme for a lighter-than-air flying machine. Like an ordinary ship, it had a hull, mast, and sail, but it was also furnished with four large hollow spheres made of thinly beaten copper. The idea was that when all the air was pumped out of the spheres, they would be left lighter than the surrounding atmosphere and lift the ship into the air. In theory, this was sound, but in practice, air pressure would have crushed the fragile copper spheres flat if a vacuum had been produced inside them. De Lana was aware of this difficulty, but thought quite wrongly that the strength of the spherical shape would prevent their being damaged.

This airship might seem primitive, but it does show real and constructive thought. For one thing, de Lana realized that ballast would be needed to control the ascent. It would be thrown overboard until the ship was just light 47

The Sovereign of the Seas *of 1637 carried an unusually large spread of canvas for her day.*

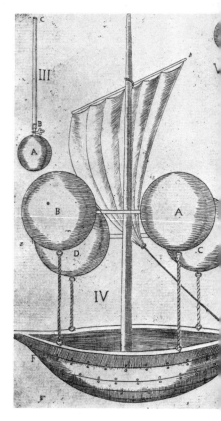

Francesco de Lana's flying ship design of 1670.

enough to lift gently off the water. The vessel would be brought down again by letting air gradually re-enter the spheres so that the ship would sink slowly back to sea-level. If it had not been for the insuperable difficulty of air pressure, there is no reason why the design should not have worked perfectly.

However, de Lana was a theorist and had no wish to build an actual airship. Besides, he clearly foresaw the military implications of flight and thought that God's displeasure would surely light on the maker of such a machine. How could the manufacture of flying ships be allowed, he argued, since once they were built, no ship at sea nor any city behind its protective walls would be free from the threat of surprise attack from the air?

Despite his miscalculations regarding the copper spheres, de Lana's ship was a great milestone. His descriptive powers and logical thought fired the imaginations of many later inventors and made his design one of the most famous in the whole of aeronautical history.

5

The Eighteenth Century

During the eighteenth century the Industrial Revolution began in England. There was a movement of people to the towns, and factories replaced single craftsmen and cottage labourers. As the century went on, steam engines, which had been invented at the end of the seventeenth century, were perfected and used increasingly to turn the machinery in the new factories. Great industrial towns grew up around the coalfields of the north and the midlands, and these needed new means of transport to carry in the raw materials and take out the finished products.

Even at the beginning of the eighteenth century England's inland transport system was inadequate. The method of road making was still very primitive. Earth was dug from drainage ditches at the sides of the roads and piled in the middle, in the hope that passing vehicles would compress it into a reasonably hard surface. Sometimes gravel was sprinkled on, more or less as an afterthought. In some areas the method worked well enough, but where clay came to the surface, it was a different story. Here rainwater did not drain away quickly, and after a storm the road was soon worked into an almost impassable pudding of sticky mud in which horses sank up to their bellies and carts up to their wheel hubs.

Stagecoach passengers journeying between the major cities had to put up with great discomfort and endless delays. In 1774, for instance, the London to Glasgow coach took ten days under good conditions, but often the journey extended to two weeks. The timetable was so uncertain that a gun had to be fired to let people know when the coach had arrived.

In America the roads were even worse, and long-distance travel relied mainly on the sea and navigable rivers. The few roads which existed before the Revolution did not link the colonies together, but served only their own localities. When independence had been won, efforts were made to improve road communications between the newly formed states. Stagecoaches began to run between the main towns, but roads were so bad that it took a week to get from Boston to New York. Pioneers heading West still travelled along the rivers.

*The Bath Mail Coach of 1784 was the first stagecoach to carry the royal mail.
Notice the primitive road surface.*

The French led the way to better roads. From 1764 onward, Trésaguet was building across France roads which had firm foundations of stone blocks, thick coverings of coarsely broken rocks, and surfaces of small stones. These roads were arched, or cambered, to allow drainage, and bounded by curbstones. They were the wonder of Europe and, before long, were imitated by other countries.

The first British roads made in the same way were built by the remarkable blind engineer John Metcalfe. Born in Yorkshire, in 1717, he went blind when only six. Despite this handicap, he was full of confidence, walked about freely by himself, and even learned to ride a horse well enough to go hunting. In 1765 he won a contract to make a three-mile stretch of road from Harrogate to Boroughbridge in Yorkshire, and followed Trésaguet's method of construction. Metcalfe's experiment was so successful that other orders for road making flowed in, and altogether he built about 180 miles of Yorkshire toll road.

In general, however, British roads still could not cope with the country's increasing trade. Rivers were used whenever possible, and in the seventeenth century some previously unnavigable rivers had been opened up to barges by the deepening of their channels. It was not until the middle of the eighteenth century, however, that the first industrialized canals were dug. The most successful of these early waterways was completed in 1761 on the orders of the Duke of Bridgewater. It linked the duke's coal mines at Worsley to Manchester, 10 miles away and allowed the raw material to be brought cheaply into the manufacturing centre.

The original canal was so successful that the duke extended it to connect with the River Mersey, thus allowing free access for Manchester's goods to the thriving port of Liverpool.

The Bridgewater canal made a great deal of money for the duke, but more important, it encouraged the digging of many more waterways. An efficient interconnecting system of canals grew up and provided the arteries along which the lifeblood of industrial England flowed.

Canals were not the only new method of transportation. During the latter part of the seventeenth century, railways emerged from underground mine workings and were built to carry freight on the surface. By the eighteenth century such railways were quite common in the mining districts of Durham and Northumberland, where they were used to carry coal from the minehead to the riverside. Initially, the rails along which horses dragged the heavily laden coal carts were made of wood. These rails wore down very quickly and were usually repaired merely by nailing another plank on top of the worn section. At bends, however, the wear and tear was particularly bad, and iron plates were sometimes laid on top of the rails to give added protection. After a while it became the custom to plate the entire length of wooden track with sheets of iron. Railways of this sort were called plateways. The problem of wear was now transferred from the rails to the wooden wagon wheels, which lasted no time on the hard metal-covered tracks. By the 1750's the answer had been found, and wheels were cast out of solid iron.

Even now the difficulties of railway operators were not over. As the iron-wheeled wagons rumbled and clattered over the track, nails worked loose, and the iron rail plates tilted or fell off. The solution this time was found in rails which were made completely of iron. It is not known who first used cast-iron rails, but it is certain that several tons of them were made in 1767 at the great Coalbrookdale Ironworks in Shropshire and that a track was laid down at the works itself. These rails had an inner flange, which stopped the plain wheeled wagons from jumping the track. A serious defect was that the rails sometimes broke under heavy trucks, but after reductions in wagon size, the system worked very well.

More and more iron tracks were laid, but they did not begin to predominate over wood until the last decade of the century. Many of these 51

The Barton Aqueduct carrying the Bridgewater Canal over the River Irwell. In its day the aqueduct was regarded as one of the wonders of the world.

newer wagonways used flanged wheels and edge rails in the way that railways do to this day.

During the eighteenth century, railways and canals worked in conjunction. Tracks led from mines and factories down to the canal banks, where wagons could unload into waiting barges. Railways were for short journeys, while canal barges carried the freight for longer distances. Not many people can have foreseen, as the century closed, that in a few years the great canal system would be largely superseded by the seemingly insignificant railways.

Steam was the secret of the railways' success. As soon as the first steam engines appeared, men began to dream of using them to propel land vehicles and boats. There were many experiments during the eighteenth century, and although none of them was commercially successful, they did pave the way for the great developments in mechanical transport which occurred in the nineteenth century.

The first steam road vehicle was made in 1769 by the French military engineer Nicholas Cugnot. It was a great cumbersome tricycle, which could manage a speed of just over 2 mph for the quarter of an hour that its steam supply lasted.

Inventors were also active in Britain and America. An American, Oliver Evans, produced a steam-driven coach in the 1770's but had little success, partly because of the bad state of the roads. The experiments of the Englishmen Fourness and Ashworth were cut short for a different reason. They built an interesting little steam-powered four-wheeler in 1788, but unfortunately, Fourness died suddenly, so the design was not developed.

Other men took steam power onto the water. The most successful of these

52

early experimenters was the French Marquis de Jouffroy. His steamboat *Pyroscaphe* was 140 feet long and was driven by steam-operated paddle wheels. Several experimental runs were attempted, and in 1783 *Pyroscaphe*'s engine proved powerful enough to drive the 182-ton ship upstream against the full force of the Saône near Lyon, in central France.

An even more important figure in the development of the steamboat was the Scotsman, William Symington. He got into the business accidentally when he was asked to install an engine to drive the paddles of a strange twin-hulled vessel built by his fellow Scot Patrick Miller. Trials took place in 1788 on Dalswinton Loch. With its two steam-driven paddle wheels churning between the catamaranlike hulls, the little 25-foot craft crossed the lake at the brisk speed of 5 mph and, much to the spectators' surprise and disappointment, failed to burst its boiler. In 1789 a more powerful engine was fitted and a speed of 7 mph was achieved on a run along the Forth and Clyde Canal. About this time, Miller became dissatisfied and dropped out of the picture. Symington went on experimenting by himself and in the early years of the next century produced a really operable steamer.

America, too, had its steamboat pioneers. William Henry experimented with steam-driven models as early as 1770 and supplied the inspiration which led John Fitch to build a full-size boat in 1786. Fitch actually formed a company to operate steamboat services on the Delaware River, but the enterprise was ahead of its time and never made money.

Steam power was not the only dream of the future to exercise men's imaginations. There were also those whose thoughts soared into the air, and in the late eighteenth century the secret of flight was at last discovered. The nature of the secret would have surprised the tower jumpers and bird-men of earlier times, for the first man to fly floated gently aloft on a cloud of hot air, with none of the furious flapping of wings that those old experimenters had expected.

The two men who showed the world how to fly were the brothers Mont-golfier from provincial France. By profession they were paper manufacturers at the little town of Annonay near Lyon, but by inclination they were scientists with a particular interest in gases. One day the elder brother, Joseph, was sitting in front of a fire when he noticed fragments of ash being carried up by the current of hot air rising from the flames. This gave him the idea of catching the gas given off by the fire in some sort of bag. With the help of his younger brother, Étienne, Joseph set about his first experiment. A small fire was kindled indoors, and a silk bag held above it to collect the fumes. The bag swelled as it filled with hot air, lifted, and then floated gently to the ceiling. With increasing excitement and enthusiasm, the   53

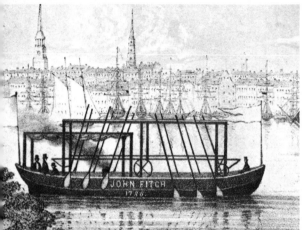

Top: *In the 18th century, mine railways came a..
ground. The picture shows the Parkmoor wagon..
near Newcastle, in 1783.*
Above left: *John Fitch's steam paddle-boat on..
Delaware River in 1786.*
Above right: *Miller and Symington's double-hu..
steamboat on Dalswinton Loch, Scotland, in 1788*
Left: *Cugnot's road steamer of 1769–70 wa..
tricycle that could lumber along at about 2 mph.*
Below: *The French Marquis de Jouffroy's steam..
Pyroscaphe of 1783 was powerful enough to r..
her way upstream against the full force of the Saône R..
near Lyon.*

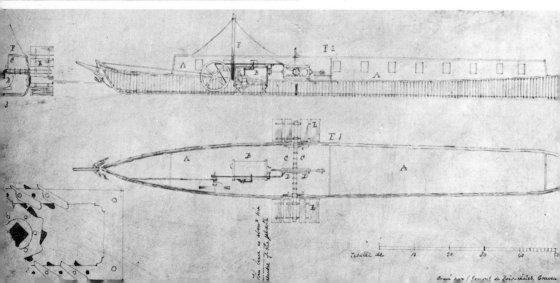

Montgolfiers busied themselves with still further tests and in June, 1783, were confident enough to demonstrate an unmanned balloon before their fellow townsmen of Annonay.

News of the ascent quickly spread across France and reached the famous Académie des Sciences in Paris. The members of the Académie were torn between doubt and belief, and they decided to commission one of their number, the physicist Jacques Alexandre Charles, to try to make a balloon himself. Charles had no idea what gas the Montgolfiers had used to obtain buoyancy, so he settled on hydrogen as the lightest material known.

By a fortunate accident, two other brothers, the Robert, had just perfected a method of rubberizing silk, which made it an ideal fabric to contain hydrogen. Charles engaged them to make a balloon to his design. It was a globe of about 13 feet in diameter and had a filling tube at the bottom through which the gas could enter. In August, 1783, the balloon was inflated with hydrogen, and released from the Champ de Mars in Paris. Despite poor weather, a large crowd had assembled and was enthusiastically impressed when the unmanned device rose and disappeared into the low clouds after remaining visible for about two minutes.

There is an amusing sequel. After drifting for about fifteen miles, the balloon descended on the sleepy little village of Gonesse, whose inhabitants had heard nothing of the experiment. With horror, the villagers watched the globe drop out of the sky and come bouncing toward them over the fields and hedges. Some thought it was a visitor from another world, others that it was a giant bird; all were terror-stricken. Gradually they took courage from their number and the balloon's inactivity and closed in with extreme caution. At last a particularly bold villager let fly with his gun. The balloon slowly subsided, and with a cry of triumph, the rest rushed in, brandishing flails and pitchforks, intent on the kill. As the fabric was ripped open, out rushed the hydrogen gas, causing such a stench that the crowd retreated more quickly than it had advanced. But by now the balloon was such a sorry sight that the villagers quickly regained their courage. They tied the cause of all the alarm to a horse's tail, and the rider galloped it across country until the first hydrogen balloon was torn to ignominious shreds.

During this time Étienne Montgolfier had come up to Paris and was busy making a large Montgolfière, or hot-air balloon, in the garden of a fellow paper manufacturer. After a successful test, this balloon was demonstrated to members of the Académie, but on both occasions the device was tethered so that it could not blow away.

Étienne's next step was to give a demonstration before Louis XVI and Marie Antoinette in September, 1783. For the first time, the balloon carried 55

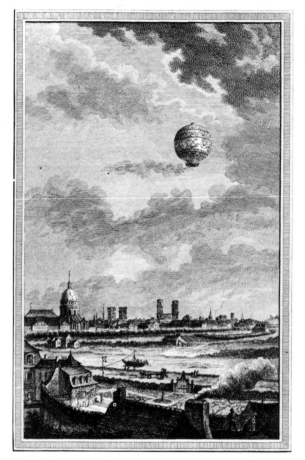

passengers—a sheep, a rooster, and a duck, which were suspended in a cage from the bottom of the envelope, the bag which contained the gas. The ascent went without a hitch, and $1\frac{1}{2}$ miles were covered before the balloon came to earth again. The animals inside would have been completely unharmed if the sheep had not lashed out with its hooves and damaged the rooster's wing. His Majesty was so pleased with the display that he made the Montgolfier family members of the nobility.

Since the animals had suffered no harm from the actual flight, it was obvious that an ascent with human passengers should be attempted. The balloon used before the royal family was recovered and modified by the building of a wickerwork platform around its open neck. A brazier was fitted beneath the opening so that fuel could be burned in flight to give extra lift if it were needed.

By early October all that remained was to select the crew from the many volunteers. The authorities were reluctant to allow valuable citizens to risk their lives and wanted convicts to be sent up first. It took considerable argument to persuade the officials to change their attitude, but eventually they agreed that criminals were not worthy of such a great honour.

The most persistent of the volunteers had been the physician Pilâtre de Rozier, and it was he who was now chosen. His first ascent was on October 15, 1783, and consisted of a tethered flight in which the balloon was let up to a height of more than 80 feet by helpers on the ground. De Rozier maintained himself at this height for four minutes by burning a few handfuls of fuel on the brazier and then descended gently to earth. A huge crowd had watched the performance, fully expecting dire consequences, and when the first pilot stepped from his platform, he was greeted with amazed hero-

The first piloted hydrogen balloon ascent, December 1, 1783.

worship. Several more tethered flights were made to steadily increasing heights.

Now that the balloon was proved and the pilot trained, the time had come for the first free flight. The gardens of the royal Château de la Muette had been made available for the great occasion, and on November 21, 1783, de Rozier, the pilot, and his passenger, the Marquis d'Arlandes, climbed aboard the wickerwork platform. The fire under the balloon was stoked, and the great shape filled with hot air; it surged upward as the tethering ropes were released. For twenty-five minutes the balloon drifted on the breeze, passing over Paris, crossing the Seine, and travelling a total of about $5\frac{1}{2}$ miles. Finally, it sank gently to earth and both de Rozier and d'Arlandes scrambled out unhurt.

The momentous year of 1783 was to see another, and perhaps more important, ascent. After his first success Professor Charles wanted to build a larger man-carrying hydrogen balloon. The brothers Robert again undertook the construction. Charles' design was brilliant. The spherical envelope was $27\frac{1}{2}$ feet in diameter and made up of gores of rubberized silk, coloured alternately red and yellow. At the bottom of the balloon was a filling tube and, at the top, a valve to allow gas to escape when the aeronauts wished to descend. A net over the top half of the envelope supported a circular hoop from which was hung the basket for the crew. Ballast was to be carried, which could be jettisoned to lighten the balloon.

When complete, the balloon was transported to the Tuileries Gardens on December 1, 1783. The rubberized envelope was slung between poles and inflated with hydrogen gas, made on the spot by the action of dilute sulphuric acid on iron filings. Several hours were needed to produce enough gas, but eventually the balloon was filled and moved out into the open, away from the shelter of a clump of trees, where the inflation had taken place. Charles and the elder Robert embarked, taking with them a barometer and a thermometer and also sand to use as ballast. At the professor's signal, the restraining ropes were cast off, and the balloon shot up.

The flight lasted two hours, and in that time the balloon drifted about 27 miles before coming down at Nelse. Here Robert got out, but Charles decided to go up again, probably to take some more readings with his scientific instruments. Unfortunately, no suitable ballast could be found to make up for the loss of his companion's weight, so as soon as Charles gave the order to cast off again, the balloon streaked upward. As it rose, the pressure of the air around it fell. The gas inside the balloon began to expand, threatening to burst the envelope. Desperately Charles released gas through the crown valve and the filling tube, and at last the wild ascent was halted,

Monamy Swaine's painting of H.M.S. Victory, *Admiral Lord Nelson's flagship at the Battle of Trafalgar, 1805.*

but not before a height of 9,000 feet was reached and the ground was completely hidden by banks of clouds. The scientist still had composure enough to take notes on the readings of his instruments and then to descend to make a perfect landing. In his writings he comments chiefly on the extreme cold and the intense pain he felt in his eardrums, but the whole experience must have been so terrifying that it is hardly surprising that Charles never flew again.

After the successes of 1783, ballooning became a fashionable craze. Many balloons of both the Charlesière and Montgolfière types were made, but the more efficient hydrogen-filled Charlesière soon began to predominate. Eventually, when it became obvious that balloons were at the mercy of the wind and could never be really practical vehicles of travel, enthusiasm waned. The start of the Napoleonic Wars caused interest in ballooning to dwindle even more, and although the French did use a few captive balloons

59

for reconnaissance in the early stages of the war, they soon went out of service.

But if lighter-than-air devices were in temporary decline, developments were afoot that would eventually lead to the aeroplane. The man who led the science of flight out of its dark age of feather flapping was the Englishman Sir George Cayley. This country gentleman, who lived from 1773 to 1857, probably had his interest kindled in boyhood by the balloon pioneers. His first success was a model helicopter which was made and flown when he was about twenty-three; later he realized that the problem of flight was, to quote his own words, "to make a surface support a given weight by the application of power to the resistance of air." In the next century he continued his important work, but that story must wait until a later chapter.

The foundations were already being laid for the bewildering developments of the nineteenth and twentieth centuries, but the everyday transport of the eighteenth century was slow to alter. Although the use of canals and railways was expanding, the horse still held first place on land, while at sea the sail was as yet unchallenged.

By the eighteenth century, in fact, sailing ships had been brought to such a state of perfection that further great improvements seemed almost impossible. Already a first-rater like Nelson's *Victory* could carry about six times as much sail as a Tudor warship, and her burden of 2,332 tons was about as big as a wooden vessel could safely be. Design was almost static, as the *Victory* herself showed. She was launched in 1765, and forty years later, during the Napoleonic Wars, she was still considered good enough to act as Lord Nelson's flagship. There were occasional innovations. Copper sheathing was introduced to protect the wooden ships from rotting below the waterline, and another change was the adoption of the helmsman's wheel to control the rudder. There was even wild talk of making iron ships, but no right-thinking seaman took that idea seriously.

Despite the fact that there was little development apparent on either land or sea, much was actually learned in the eighteenth century, and many new ideas were tried out. The harvest is still being reaped in our own era of technological progress.

6

The Nineteenth Century: 1 Early Railways and Roads

The nineteenth century changed the face of the earth. By the time it ended, railways spanned the continents, petrol-engined cars drove on the roads, and large steamers plied every ocean. Controllable airships had flown, and genuine heavier-than-air flight was only a few years away. It was a century of achievement and activity, when all were confident in the inevitability and desirability of material progress.

Two great changes revolutionized land transport at the beginning of the nineteenth century. One was the coming of practical steam-driven vehicles, and the other was the development of public railways.

In 1801 Richard Trevithick, a young mining engineer, from Cornwall, England, built a passenger vehicle for use on the roads. It was tested on Christmas Eve, and except for a tendency of the boiler to run dry, it worked very well. The inventor and his friends were extremely pleased with the carriage and celebrated by making sure that they themselves did not run short of liquid refreshment. Three days after the original tests, the vehicle was left parked outside an inn while Trevithick and his cronies went inside, still in a festive mood. The engine's thirst was quite forgotten, and when the drinkers finally rushed out, the boiler had run dry, and the whole carriage was in flames.

Trevithick was a stouthearted Cornishman and took the setback in his stride. Before long, another steamcoach was finished and ready for testing. This time the engineer felt able to face a larger audience, so in 1803 he decided to take his machine up to London. While in the capital, he made a successful run between the London boroughs of Holborn and Paddington, but neither the public nor the highways were ready for mechanical road transport, so the young inventor turned his thoughts in another direction.

Railways were familiar to him from his work as a mining engineer, and their smooth, even tracks seemed to offer just the conditions his steam engines needed. With this in mind, Trevithick persuaded the owner of the

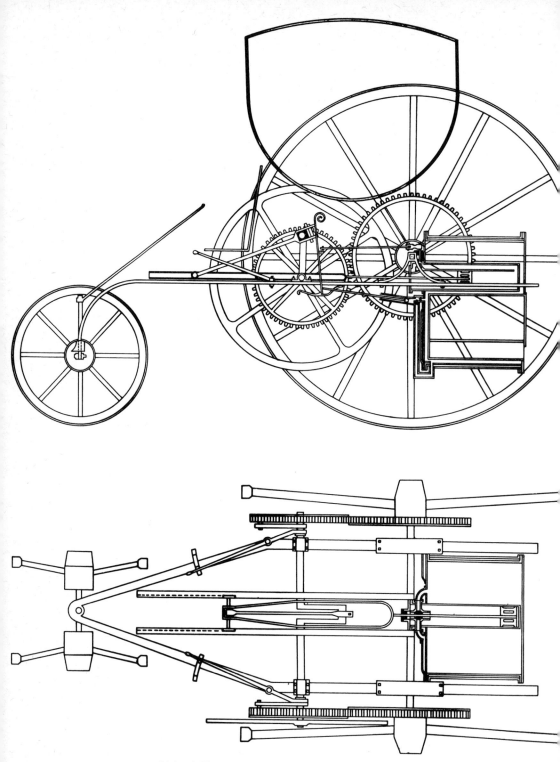

Richard Trevithick's patent drawing for a steam carriage, 1802.

Pen-y-darran ironworks in Wales to let him build a locomotive to haul iron along the 10-mile tramway that led from the works in Merthyr Tydfil to the head of a canal in Abercynon. The Pen-y-darran engine was first tested on February 11, 1804. Later it made several journeys along the length of the track, and on one occasion it hauled five wagons loaded with ten tons of iron and seventy men at 5 mph. This showed that the locomotive's wheels would give enough grip to enable heavy loads to be moved, but the experiments had to be ended, because the five-ton engine kept breaking the brittle cast-iron rails.

Trevithick was still full of confidence in the future of steam locomotion and built other improved engines. He took one of these to London in 1808 for a series of demonstrations intended to arouse public interest and curiosity. A circular track was set up near Euston Road, and the engine Catch Me Who Can was used for joyriding at five shillings a trip. The little railway did a roaring trade until a derailment shattered confidence and dried up the supply of customers overnight.

The first commercially successful locomotive was designed by John Blenkinsop and used from 1812 onward in the Middleton colliery near Leeds. Four of its six wheels were smooth-rimmed and ran on the ordinary track, but the two driving wheels had teeth which engaged on rack rails to ensure a good grip.

Much more famous was William Hedley's Puffing Billy which appeared in 1813 and ran between Wylam colliery and Lemington-on-Tyne for nearly fifty years. Its inventor found, as Trevithick already had, that smooth wheels gave enough purchase on the rails to move even heavily laden wagons, so he was able to avoid the extra expense of a rack system like that of Blenkinsop. There was, however, the same old difficulty of the cast iron rails breaking under the weight of the engine. Hedley thought of a simple solution to this problem. He just gave his locomotive four extra wheels so that its weight would be more evenly distributed. This modification lasted from 1815 till 1830, when the 5-mile-long track was relaid with wrought-iron rails, which were strong enough to allow the number of wheels to be reduced to the original four.

George Stephenson (1781–1848) was the most important of the railway pioneers, but he did not produce his first engine till 1814, and even that was not a complete success. However, the inventor had come up the hard way and knew how to persevere. His youth had been spent in poverty, and he had even had to teach himself to read and write. The turning point in his life had come in 1812, when his skill with machinery had earned him the job of enginewright at the High Pit colliery near Killingworth. His second engine

Trevithick's circular railroad near Euston Road, London.

Blenkinsop's locomotive of 1812. The two driving wheels had teeth which engaged in rack rails.

The opening of the Stockton and Darlington Railway, 1825. Taken from a contemporary sketch.

Pioneers heading west in ox-drawn wagons. When the Cumberland road was extended through Ohio and Indiana into Illinois during the mid-19th century, it replaced the rivers as the chief route for westward migration.

appeared in 1815 and was made for use at his employer's mine. This time the locomotive worked well and was followed by a whole series of Killingworth engines which enabled Stephenson to build up invaluable experience in the design and maintenance of all kinds of railway equipment.

By 1823 Stephenson was such an acknowledged expert on railway construction and engine design that he was the natural choice for the post of surveyor and engineer of the proposed Stockton-Darlington line. This was only 10 miles long, but when it was officially opened on September 17, 1825, it became the first public steam-operated railway to carry both passengers and freight, so it has an important place in the history of travel.

The inaugural trip was greeted with great enthusiasm. Stephenson's engine *Active*, or *Locomotion*, as it was later called, pulled the train, and the famous engineer himself acted as driver. There were thirty-three wagons in all, crammed with freight and passengers. The train set out amid scenes of tremendous excitement, with about 450 people on board. So great was the interest that many others ran along beside the wagons and jumped on whenever the engine slowed down. This was not too difficult, since the top speed was only 12 mph, and by the time the journey finished, there were 150 extra passengers.

Subsequently, there were technical difficulties, although the little railway always more than paid its way. During the first two years of operation the locomotives often broke down, so that the running of the line had frequently to be taken over by horses. The superiority of steam was not finally proved until the introduction in 1827 of a reliable new engine, Hackworth's *Royal George*.

In the meantime, Stephenson worked hard to improve his designs, and by 1829, when the new Liverpool and Manchester Railway held a competitive trial for engines, he was able to come up with a winner. Four engines in all took part in the Rainhill Trials, a fifth entry having been disqualified when a horse was found inside it. Stephenson's famous *Rocket* proved to be the outstanding success. It was by far the most reliable engine and was able to do a victory run at the unheard of speed of nearly 30 mph. Many spectators, in fact, thought that the locomotive was travelling so fast that the rush of air had killed the driver, a man called Dickson. The engine seemed to be careering headlong to disaster, so the relief and applause was intense when Dickson halted the train in front of the grandstand and jumped down unharmed. After this convincing win, there was no doubt whose engines would run on the Liverpool and Manchester Railway. The design team of George Stephenson and his son Robert supplied the *Rocket* and seven other similar locomotives, which, from 1830 onward, operated the first really regular passenger service in the world.

Mechanics' Magazine,

MUSEUM, REGISTER, JOURNAL, AND GAZETTE.

No. 324.]   SATURDAY, OCTOBER 24, 1829.   [Price 3*d*.

"THE ROCKET," LOCOMOTIVE STEAM ENGINE OF
MR. ROBERT STEPHENSON.

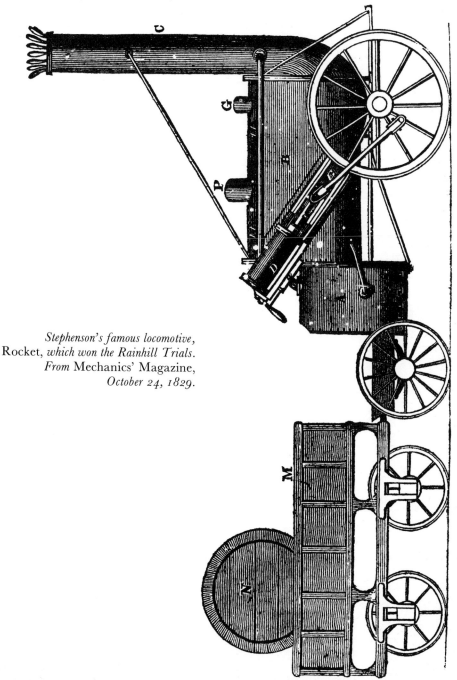

Stephenson's famous locomotive,
Rocket, *which won the Rainhill Trials.*
From Mechanics' Magazine,
October 24, 1829.

Road improvements were less spectacular than the rise of the railways, but a new way of making good roads, devised by the Scotsman John McAdam, had a far-reaching beneficial effect. McAdam was born in 1756, went to the United States as a boy, but returned to Britain in 1783.

His method of road building was quicker and cheaper than Trésaguet's. The top soil was simply dug away, and a layer of broken stones 10 inches to 1 foot thick was then spread on. There was no expensive stone block foundation. All that was necessary was to break up the stones until they were roughly 1 inch in diameter and to ensure good drainage. After traffic had passed over the road for a time, the stones settled into a continuous sheet which could easily support the weight of a wagon. McAdam never really understood why this happened. He was content just to use the effect. Actually it worked in this way: passing wheels ground dust off the stones, and the dust mixed with rainwater and worked its way into the spaces between the stones, so that the whole road surface became cemented together.

McAdam's roads became world-famous. American engineers who had studied his methods returned home and macadamized the great Cumberland Road east of the Ohio River. The Cumberland Road was the United States' first national highway. In 1818 it had linked Maryland and Virginia. By 1852 it had been extended to 834 miles and stretched on through Ohio, Indiana, and into Illinois. It replaced the rivers as the main avenue for Western migration, and its length was thronged by the covered wagons of the pioneers.

Improvements in the roads and the triumph of railway locomotives encouraged several British inventors to try their hands at steam road carriages. One of the best known was the Cornishman Sir Goldsworthy Gurney, whose design work started in 1823. Two years later he patented a steam-carriage propelled by pushing legs, but he soon abandoned this strange idea. During the years 1827 and 1828 he produced a steam stagecoach, which was run in the neighbourhood of London for about two years. This coach had four main wheels and two smaller steering wheels in front. It was big enough to hold eighteen passengers but could still achieve the very creditable speed of 15 mph.

Gurney's later coaches were improved by reducing their weight, while keeping the same driving power, but despite all his efforts, they remained unreliable and often broke down. Even when his steam coaches did manage to keep moving, their passengers enjoyed little about the ride other than the novelty, for they were jolted and bumped, half-fried, and often engulfed in smoke. As if these hazards were not enough, one of the steamers was actually attacked in 1829 by an angry antimachinery mob.

One of Hancock's steam coaches, 1833.

A Gurney steam carriage approaching Highgate Tunnel in the London suburbs, late 1820's.

In 1831 Sir Charles Dance bought all Gurney's remaining coaches and put them to work carrying passengers between Gloucester and Cheltenham, in the west of England. The vehicles averaged 12 mph for this 9-mile route, even allowing for stops to pick up fares, but sabotage and propaganda by local innkeepers and stagecoach lines frightened customers, so that Sir Charles was soon driven out of business.

Walter Hancock, another steam carriage enthusiast, made his first coach, a small three-wheeler, in 1829. A much more successful four-wheeled steamer followed, and in February, 1831, Hancock was able to open the first scheduled passenger service ever to use a self-propelled road vehicle. His coach, *Infant*, thundered from Stratford, Essex, to London reaching 15 mph on level stretches even with all its 14 seats filled.

But perhaps Hancock's greatest triumph came in 1836 when he was able to maintain regular passenger services in the London suburbs for twenty whole weeks. During that time his three coaches, *Autopsy*, *Erin* and *Automaton* travelled between them 4,000 miles and carried 13,000 passengers. However, none of the coaches was well enough sprung to give a comfortable ride, and the boilers gave off unpleasant fumes and too much heat. Once the novelty had worn off, there was little to attract the public, and the services finally had to be withdrawn for lack of support. Hancock persevered with the *Automaton* till 1840, but then high road tolls and shortage of money forced him to give up.

Interest in steam carriages waned and, in Britain, it was almost extinguished by a law of 1865, which limited speeds to 2 mph in towns and decreed that a man with a red flag should march at least 60 yards in front of any mechanically driven vehicle to warn of its approach.

Railways did not suffer from any of the difficulties of road steamers. They went from strength to strength as the nineteenth century progressed. The old, established countries of Europe gained great benefits from them, while the new, emerging nations of the Americas could hardly have come into being without their existence.

In Europe the main effect of the railways was to increase trade and strengthen industrial economies. The cost of transportation was sharply decreased, and goods could be moved quickly and cheaply across land. Mineral resources were made increasingly accessible as more and more tracks led into and out of the mining regions. The dramatic changes that a railway could bring are illustrated by the figures for coal shipped out of Stockton before and after the Stockton-Darlington Railway was built. In 1822, before the line was opened, Stockton exported 1,224 tons of coal. By 1828 only three years after the railway had started operations, the figure had risen to 66,051 tons. Other factors were probably at work, but the increase must have been due largely to the railway.

Until railways came along, many canals had enjoyed a monopoly in the carrying trade and had raised their charges to an unfair level. Competition with railway lines brought the freight rates tumbling down, and soon many canals were in financial trouble. The new railways were faster and more reliable and efficient. On the canals, goods could be held stationary for weeks by frost, drought, or even floods. Furthermore, pilfering was widespread on the barges. Canals really did not stand a chance. Railways even had a psychological advantage—they were modern and seemed to embody the very spirit of progress. People were anxious to use them. Not surprisingly, canal traffic was reduced to a tiny fraction of the total goods in transit.

If railways were important in Europe, they were even more vital to the development of the huge new countries of North and South America and the gigantic Russian Empire. The iron lines were the stitches which sewed these vast territories into nations.

Railroads started early in the United States. The first one, the Baltimore and Ohio, was opened in 1830 and worked by horses and even sails before a definite decision in favour of steam was made in 1831. Several other railroads   71

A Pony Express rider—member of the swiftest long-distance postal service which the world had yet seen.

The Best Friend of Charlesto[n] *1830, was the first United Sta[tes] steam locomotive to be used on scheduled passenger service.*

came into operation at about the same time, and one connecting Charleston and Hamburg in South Carolina was the first in America to use a steam engine, the *Best Friend*, on a scheduled passenger run. The rate of progress was so high that by 1840 there were almost 3,000 miles of track in the United States, and this had extended to more than 30,000 miles when the Civil War broke out in 1861.

The Civil War convinced Congress that communications had to be improved if the country were to be held together. Hostile Indians and difficult terrain made overland travel between the East and the Far West insecure and perilous. William Fargo of the American Express Company had pioneered coach travel from the Mississippi River, through Texas and New Mexico, to San Francisco in 1858, but the long sea route around Cape Horn remained the major link between the Atlantic and Pacific coasts. A year or so later the Pony Express had brought San Francisco to within nine days' travelling time of New York. Relays of riders carried mail West from Missouri, changing horses about every 15 miles and riding like fury every inch of the way. It was the swiftest long-distance postal service that the world had yet seen, but at $10 an ounce, it was extremely expensive. Politicians and businessmen looked to the railroads to provide a surer route to the West.

At the height of the Civil War, the courageous decision was made to go ahead with a transcontinental railroad. Rails were to follow the old Mormon Trail into Utah and meet a track being driven inland from the West Coast. "The work of giants," as General Sherman called it, began on January 8,

1863, and was completed by the ceremonial driving of the last spike on May 10, 1869.

Two companies took part in the historic enterprise. The Central Pacific Railroad Company started from Sacramento in the West eleven months before its counterpart, the Union Pacific Railroad, began to lay track west from Omaha on the Missouri River.

There were daunting difficulties to be faced. Within 70 miles of its starting point, the Western company had to begin the laborious climb over the granite mountains of the Sierra Nevada. The workmen, many of them Chinese, were still in the forbidding region, bridging gorges and painstakingly chipping tunnels through the hard rock, when they were overtaken by the ferocious winter of 1866–67. There was snow on the Sierras from November till April, and the tunnels were the only places where work could continue. Even the tunnelling was hampered because the intense cold made tools so brittle that they broke easily. There was seldom more than a foot of progress in twenty-four hours.

To begin with, the Union Pacific was much more fortunate. The beginning of its route lay through pleasant farmland and prairie, but it, too, had its deserts and mountains to negotiate. Before it lay the Rockies, the Black Hills, and the Wasatch range, and as the workmen pressed on out of the settled regions, there was the ever-present danger of hostile Indians—the Sioux and Cheyenne.

Through all the difficulties, both companies performed prodigies of ingenuity and endurance. When their tracks met on Promontory Point in Utah, they had completed the world's first transcontinental railroad, spanning 1,800 miles in about half the time allotted them by Congress.

The decades from 1870 to 1890 were the great age of railway construction in the United States. In those twenty years the astonishing total of 140,000 miles of railroad was laid. It was these railways which opened up the country for development. Often they were built before there was any traffic to use them. Freight, passengers, and progress followed in the wake of the lines.

As railway systems spread across the face of the world, improvements in locomotive design more than kept up with the rate of progress. The size and power of engines steadily increased, and speeds leaped upward. Only twenty years after the *Rocket*'s modest 30 mph had seemed unbelievable, locomotives were averaging more than 50 mph for the journey from London to Bristol, 110 miles away. The advance in performance continued, and in 1893 an American engine of the Empire State Express was able to set up a record speed of $112\frac{1}{2}$ mph. Even the dominance of steam did not go unchallenged, and before the end of the century, electrically powered locomotives

A United States locomotive of the period just after the Civil War.

The Golden Spike ceremony to mark the meeting of the Central Pacific and Union Pacific railroads on Promontory Point, Utah, May 10, 1869.

had appeared. From 1890 onward, electric trains ran on the London Underground, or subway. America produced the first main-line electrification. A 4-mile stretch of track which passed through a tunnel under the city of Baltimore was electrified in 1895 to overcome the problem of noise and dirt created by steam locomotives.

Improvements were not confined to the engines. The comfort of passengers was also catered for. In Europe, railway carriages had been modelled on stagecoaches. There was little room to move around or stretch one's legs. This was all very well for short journeys, but quite out of the question for the transcontinental distances of America. The United States produced open carriages patterned on the luxurious public cabins of her many river steamers. Sleeping cars, dining cars, and lavatory facilities were in use in the United States long before they appeared on European trains.

Even in the nineteenth century, surface traffic was a problem in the great cities. In 1843 a London lawyer named Charles Pearson suggested that a railway should be built through underground tunnels to ease congestion in the streets above. After years of discussion, the British Parliament approved the scheme in 1855, and the digging began in 1860. A deep open ditch was dug and spanned with brick arches, which were then covered with earth. Tracks were laid in the resulting tunnel to make the $3\frac{3}{4}$-mile-long Metropolitan Railway. The line opened in January, 1863, and despite choking smoke from the steam locomotives, it was an immediate and lasting success. In the first year alone, it carried more than 9,000,000 passengers. New underground railways were burrowed beneath London, where the electrification that started in 1890 made them cleaner and even more popular. Today London Transport operates 253 miles of track, 180 miles of which are below the surface, and carries 670,000,000 passengers in a year.

London's example was slowly followed by many other European capitals. Paris started its famous *métro* in 1898; Berlin opened its first stretch of *U-bahn* in 1902; Moscow was a late starter and had to wait until the 1930's. The earliest public subway in America was a $1\frac{1}{2}$-mile-long line opened in Boston in 1898. New York's first subway did not begin operations until 1904, mainly because of the city's previous reliance on elevated railroads, but now the system has grown into the largest in the world, with nearly 240 miles of tunnels. Every day it carries well over 3,000,000 people. Other cities in North and South America and in Japan have built underground railways, so that, all over the world, tube trains are making an important contribution toward easing traffic conditions in the crowded streets.

The opening of the South London Tube Railway in December, 1890. This was the first electrically operated underground railway.

Baker Street Station on the Metropolitan Railway, London, the world's first underground, 1863.

7

The Nineteenth Century: 2
Motor-cars, Bicycles,
Progress at Sea

The cause of most congestion in the streets nowadays is the motor-car, one of the most useful and also one of the most troublesome of man's inventions. Before there could be a motor-car, there had to be a new kind of engine. The first practical internal-combustion engine was made by the French engineer Étienne Lenoir in 1859. It was intended to turn factory machinery and ran on coal gas. The motor caused a sensation, even though it gobbled fuel so greedily that it was less efficient than contemporary steam engines. A newspaper report about it reached Nikolaus Otto, the self-educated son of a German innkeeper, and inspired him to efforts of his own. He experimented tirelessly, trying and discarding one idea after another. Eventually he had his reward. His 1867 model had a fuel consumption of only about one-fifth that of Lenoir's engine. Otto's motors established a pattern which has been followed by most subsequent internal-combustion engines.

Perhaps the first man to try out the new engines in a vehicle was the Austrian Siegfried Marcus. He started experiments in 1864 and drove a primitive car through the streets of Vienna in 1875. It was a four-wheeler powered by a single-cylinder internal-combustion engine, which was so explosively noisy that the police, much to the relief of the populace, banned the car from the roads. Marcus has had the last laugh, though. When his machine was taken out of its museum home for a demonstration run in 1950, it was still able, after all those years, to move quite easily under its own power.

A model of the car which Marcus drove through the streets of Vienna in 1875.

However, Marcus' efforts led nowhere, and the Germans Karl Benz and Gottlieb Daimler deserve to be regarded as the true originators of the motor-car, even though their experiments came later.

Daimler was at one time technical manager in Nikolaus Otto's firm and contributed to its success. He was fascinated by the possibility of mechanically driven vehicles, powered by light internal-combustion engines and

Benz' motor tricycle of 1885.

A replica of Daimler's motorcycle of 1885. The British comedian Norman Wisdom is at the controls.

carrying their own fuel supply with them. Petrol was just coming on the market from the newly exploited American oil wells, and Daimler, like several other inventors, realized its potential as an easily portable motor fuel. He produced a number of experimental petrol motors, but his ideas clashed with his employers' interests in gas engines, so that eventually he was dismissed from his position.

Daimler moved to Cannstatt, determined to justify his faith in petrol. Throughout the autumn and winter of 1883–84, a series of shattering explosions and thunderous roars issued from his workshop, disturbing the peace of the quiet district where he lived. Neighbours became anxious and indignant and once even sent for the police, but nothing could halt the inventor's feverish activity. At last an engine was perfected and fitted to a modified bicycle. This motorcycle was tested in 1885, but by then another German, Karl Benz, had driven in a petrol-powered car.

Karl Benz came from Mannheim. He was the son of one of Germany's earliest engine drivers, and a passion for mechanical transport was in his blood. His historic first car was a small tricycle powered by a single-cylinder water-cooled petrol engine of his own design. The front wheel, which was smaller than the two back ones, could be turned by a small steering wheel set in front of the bench on which the driver and passenger sat. An advanced detail was the use of a differential gear on the rear axle. This allowed the two back wheels to rotate at different speeds when they traversed inner and outer arcs as the car rounded a bend. The power of the engine was transmitted to the wheels by chains, and there was a primitive form of clutch which allowed the engine to be run in neutral. Maximum speed was about 8 mph. The inventor was so pleased with his car's performance during the first test in 1885 that he forgot what he was doing and let it run straight into a wall.

Benz made improvements and decided to show his invention to the world at the Paris Exhibition of 1887. It attracted little attention, but recognition came about a year later, when a drive through the streets of Munich caused a sensation and produced a flood of orders. When Benz returned home full of his success, he discovered that his sons, aged 15 and 13, had a triumph of their own. They had made use of their father's absence to borrow another of his cars and had calmly driven their mother from Mannheim to Pforzheim and back, a distance of 80 miles, which for those days was a record for any petrol-driven vehicle.

Daimler, meanwhile, had not been idle. In 1886 he produced a four-wheeled car which could achieve 11 mph, even though it did look like a carriage minus the horses. His 1889 model, which was shown in Paris, was much more advanced. It could seat four, had a water-cooled engine, and employed four gears. It had lost the look of a horseless carriage. It was a motor-car, a vehicle in its own right.

In the early 1890's the centre of automobile design switched to France. Two Frenchmen, René Panhard and Émile Levassor, acquired the right to manufacture Daimler engines and in 1891 began to use them in cars of their own construction. Until then, designers had placed the engine in the centre of the car and perched the passengers above it. As a result, the vehicles were top-heavy, and the passengers got hot seats. The two Frenchmen changed this by installing the engine under a hood in the front of the car. They had set a pattern followed by most vehicles to this day.

One of the very earliest American cars was made by the Duryea brothers in

1893. It had one striking peculiarity—the driver had no control over the speed. Later models by the same designers were more orthodox and won several races in the years immediately prior to 1900.

From 1895 onward, Britain and the United States began to enter the picture, and the future appearance of an English car industry was ensured by the repeal, in 1896, of the "Red Flag Law." Motorists staged a great rally to mark their release from bondage and drove in triumph from London to Brighton, 50 miles south. Even today, the event is still celebrated by the annual Veteran Car Rally over the same route.

One of the great figures in industrial history, the American Henry Ford, produced his first successful car in 1896 and sold it for $200. Its two-cylinder, 4-hp engine gave a maximum speed of 25 mph, which compared favourably with most of its European contemporaries. Ford believed that the United States, with its growing wealth and immense distances, offered an almost unlimited market for the right kind of motor vehicle. In the twentieth century he proved himself right and became one of the richest men in the world.

Bicycles as we know them today were another invention of the nineteenth century. There had been earlier two-wheeled vehicles. A type of bicycle called the *célerifère* had been invented by the French Comte de Sivrac in 1791. Its rider sat astride and pushed it along with alternate thrusts of his legs. It was guided by banking over, since neither of its wheels could be turned. People jeered at first, but it was taken up by men of fashion and enjoyed quite a vogue in France for several years. At the height of the craze it was not unusual to see elegant young gentlemen racing one another on their *vélocifères*, for so the machines had been renamed, down the Champs Elysées in Paris. However, fashions change, and during the early years of the nineteenth century the bicycle was almost forgotten. It needed a new inventor to bring it back to life.

Top left: *A Panhard of 1894.*

Centre left: *The Duryea brothers' car of 1893 was one of the earliest American automobiles. Its horse-drawn ancestry can be clearly seen.*

Bottom left: *A hobbyhorse bicycle of 1819.*

Top right: *A penny-farthing of about 1874. This type of bicycle, with its large front wheel and tiny rear one, took its name from the two British coins.*

Bottom right: *The first Brighton Rally of 1896, held to celebrate the British motorists' release from the notorious Red Flag Law.*

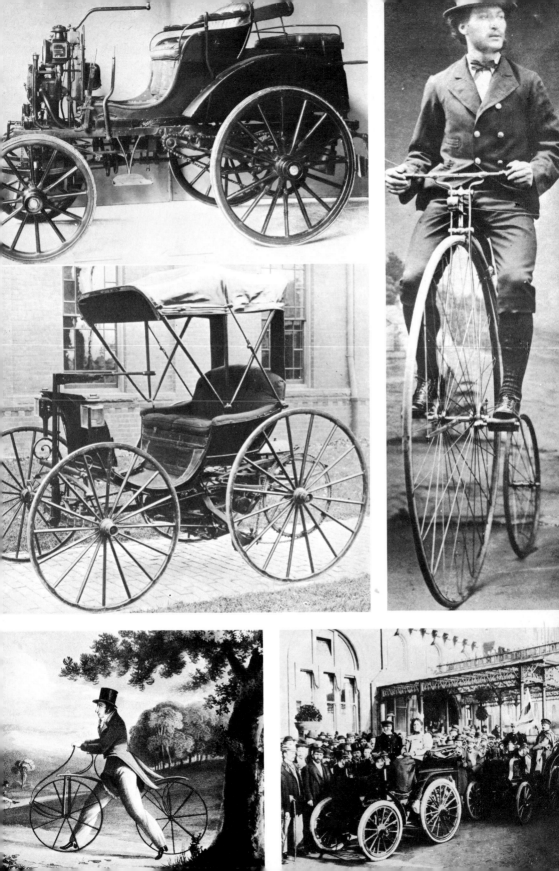

This service was performed by the eccentric German Baron Karl Friedrich Christian Ludwig von Drais de Sauerbronn, who made the first public demonstration of his so-called running machine in 1818. The baron was an agriculturalist and engineer whose work took him deep into the countryside, well away from any public transport. At first he walked, and perhaps it was on one of these long foot-slogging journeys that he first thought of modifying the *vélocifère*. His alterations were simple. He merely added a saddle and a pair of handlebars and made the front wheel swivel. Slight changes indeed, but they converted the bicycle from a toy to a useful vehicle. The new machine still had no pedals, and the driver, who sat astride, had to push himself forward with a sort of running motion. However, despite its rudimentary state, the cycle enabled the baron to cover ground quickly with little effort.

Von Drais made little or nothing from his innovations, but his improved bicycle became very popular in France, Britain, and the United States. In France it was known as a *draisienne*, while in Britain it was called a hobby-horse, or a dandy horse. Even the Prince Regent had a dandy horse, and popular support was so great in Britain and the United States that special halls were opened, where devotees of the fashion could ride in comfort. Like the craze for the *vélocifère* before it, this one, too, faded, and by 1830 the hobbyhorse was a rare sight.

The next step toward the modern bicycle was taken in 1839 by Kirkpatrick Macmillan. This Scottish blacksmith propelled his machine by pedals which were connected by rods to cranks that turned the rear wheel. Macmillan himself rode one of his machines for many years, but the type never really caught on.

In the 1860's a Frenchman called Pierre Michaux thought of connecting pedal-driven cranks to the front axle and sold so many machines that he was able to found the world's first bicycle factory.

Early Michaux bicycles had the front wheel only slightly larger than the rear. In England they were rather unkindly called boneshakers; nevertheless, they became quite popular. Even such notables as the Prince Imperial and Charles Dickens became cyclists.

Sportsmen demanded higher speeds, so during the 1870's bicycles were designed with larger front wheels, which enabled more ground to be covered for each turn of the pedals. Penny-farthings appeared, with exaggerated front wheels and tiny back ones.

Penny-farthings were speedy, but dangerous. A safer type of machine was needed for everyday use. In about 1874 the Englishman H. J. Lawson built a safety bicycle with wheels of equal size. The cranks and pedals were mounted between the wheels, and a chain led the drive to the rear axle. This form of machine was established commercially by J. K. Starley in 1885, and, after that, practically all that was needed to bring the bicycle to something resembling its modern form was good tyres.

A kind of air-filled, or pneumatic, tyre had been patented in 1845, but although some were made and fitted to coaches, there was insufficient demand for smooth-running vehicles to make production a commercial success. After being completely forgotten for many years, the idea was discovered afresh in 1887 by the Belfast veterinary surgeon, John Dunlop. According to the story, the invention came about when Dunlop's ten-year-old son wanted to win a tricycle race. To give the boy a smoother ride, Dunlop cut pieces from an old garden hose, glued them into rings, and, after pumping them full of air, fastened them to the rear wheels of the tricycle. The tyres won the race for the boy and brought the father fame and a moderate fortune. Dunlop patented his tyres in 1888 and in 1890 went into partnership with an industrialist to found the pneumatic tyre industry.

Canvas and wood to steam and iron—that was the main theme of the nineteenth century at sea. The early steamboats were fit only for sheltered inland waters, but their ironclad descendants ventured out into the oceans and drove the proud sailing ships from the sea.

The vessel that pointed the way to the future was Symington's *Charlotte Dundas*, which was, however, largely ignored when she first appeared in 1801. Her steam engine worked a single paddlewheel set in a gap left where

Symington's steamboat the Charlotte Dundas *of 1801.*

Bell's Comet *went into passenger service on the Clyde in 1812.*

Fulton's Clermont, *which began a regular steamboat service on the Hudson River in 1807.*

In 1819 the American Savannah *became the first steamship to cross the Atlantic, but most of the voyage was made under sail.*

the hull divided into two parts at the stern. She gave a very convincing performance and was the culmination of all the Scottish engineer's hopes and previous experiments. Trials were held on the Forth and Clyde Canal. The little vessel responded nobly and towed two 70-ton barges for 19 miles against a strong head wind. Symington probably hoped that the canal owners would order a fleet of steamboats, but all he got were grumbles about the effect of the steamer's wash on the canal banks. He gave up in despair and never worked on steam navigation again.

Not all those who saw the *Charlotte Dundas* were as shortsighted as the canal owners. Several witnesses went away determined to build steamers of their own. One was a visitor from the United States, a man called Robert Fulton. When he returned home, Fulton constructed the *Clermont*, which began a regular steamboat service on the Hudson River in 1807. The *Clermont* plied between New York and Albany and took on average some thirty-two hours for the 142-mile trip. When the smoke and flame of the "devil ship's" English engine were seen on the Hudson for the first time, a state of panic gripped the river users. Some just stayed where they were and prayed, while others pulled on their oars with unusual vigour and headed rapidly for the farther bank. Dread of the unknown was soon replaced by 85 fear of competition. The steamboat took their customers, so the rivermen of the Hudson retaliated with sabotage and violence. Special laws had to be enacted to control them and give the steamer a fair chance.

In 1809 another American steamship, the *Phoenix*, made a short coastal voyage from Hoboken, New Jersey, to Philadelphia. This was the first faltering step toward conquest of the open sea.

Meanwhile, in Britain, the Scot Henry Bell, another witness of Symington's demonstrations, was planning to build a steamer of his own. Long before this time, in 1800, in fact, Bell had suggested the adoption of steam by the British Admiralty. No one but Nelson treated the idea seriously, but the performance of the *Charlotte Dundas* convinced Bell anew that steam had a great future. In 1811 he launched his own vessel, the *Comet*. She was only a little ship, 43 feet long and 11 feet wide, but she was the first steamboat in Europe to have any commercial success. In addition to her steam engine, she carried sails. The mainsail, strangely enough, was not attached to a separate mast, but suspended from a yardarm, which was lashed to the tall, slender funnel.

In 1812 the *Comet* went into passenger service along the River Clyde. At first she was regarded with considerable fear and suspicion. All the grown-ups maintained that it was only a matter of time before she blew up, and all the local children trooped regularly to the riverside to await the free fireworks display. Nothing ever happened. In fact, the *Comet* made her way back and forth on the Clyde for many years and became an object of familiar affection. Her success encouraged others. Soon the Clyde shipyards were busy building her descendants.

One of these was the 38-ton *Margery*. She sailed down the coast to the River Thames, where she was rechristened *Elise*. Under this name she crossed to France to become the first steamer to conquer the English Channel.

Trips like this increased confidence in steam and encouraged the development of regular coastal services. Some of the earliest were London to Gravesend, London to Margate, Greenock to Belfast and Holyhead to Dublin, while in 1818 a Dover to Calais service was inaugurated by the 90-ton steamer *Rob Roy*.

All the early steamboats carried sails and used them whenever possible. The engines were still primitive and devoured enormous quantities of fuel. They were used only when progress was impossible under sail.

According to the "experts", steam was all right in coastal waters, but out of the question for ocean crossings. No ship could possibly carry enough coal. They were soon to be proved wrong. In 1825 two steamers, the *Falcon* and the *Enterprise* reached Calcutta via the Cape of Good Hope. The

Enterprise took 113 days, including 10 days spent coaling at various stations along the route. Long-distance steam travel was possible, but, for the time being, very expensive.

Even before this, in 1819, the American steamship *Savannah* had crossed the Atlantic, but she had been under power for only 85 hours out of a total sailing time of 27 days. Her voyage was good publicity for steam and nothing more.

Steam power did not really establish itself on the North Atlantic until 1838. In that year several ships made the entire ocean crossing with their engines in continuous operation. Competition was keen. Two passenger boats, the *Sirius* and the *Great Western*, actually arrived in New York on the same day, after being the first vessels to use steam all the way across the Atlantic. The smaller *Sirius* started from Cork in Ireland several days before her rival left Bristol, and ran so short of fuel that only 15 tons of coal remained in her bunkers when she docked. The *Great Western* was a much finer vessel and had about twice the displacement of the *Sirius*. She made the crossing in four days less than the nineteen days taken by the smaller ship.

The British Government was very impressed. The Canadian Samuel Cunard was encouraged to found the first regular transatlantic steamship line and was given an official subsidy and a contract to carry the North American mails. Cunard ordered four steam-driven sister ships from the Clyde. All were propelled by paddles, and although they were 207 feet long and displaced some 1,150 tons, they were still made of wood. The first of them, the *Britannia*, made her maiden voyage in 1840, and it was she that two years later carried the author Charles Dickens across the Atlantic. Early Cunarders had a top speed of only a little more than 8 knots, so they were frequently overtaken by sailing ships driving before a fair wind. However, the steamers could operate with a regularity that no sailing vessel could rival, so Cunard had plenty of customers.

Although the first transatlantic steamers were made of wood, iron ships had already begun to appear. The earliest of all known iron boats was a small passenger vessel that was built on the banks of the River Foss in Yorkshire in 1777. The idea took hold very slowly. People just could not accept the fact that an iron ship would float. The first iron steamer was the *Aaron Manby*, put together in London in 1821 from prefabricated pieces made in Staffordshire. Nearly two decades passed before anyone was brave enough to attempt to build a really big iron ship.

The man who took up the challenge was Isambard Kingdom Brunel, the most celebrated engineer of his day. His *Great Britain* was started in a   87

The Great Western *was the second vessel to steam all the way across the Atlantic, 1838.*

The screw-driven ship Archimedes *of 1838. After seeing her, Brunel decided to drive his new giant ship, the* Great Britain, *by means of a screw propeller.*

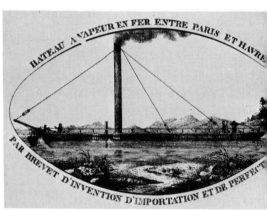

The Aaron Manby, *the first iron steamer, w built in 1821.*

The indestructible Great Britain *aground in Dundrum Bay in 1846. She was the first big iron ship, and also the first large vessel to be propelled by a screw.*

dry dock in Bristol in 1839, and four years of work were needed before she was floated in 1843. Brunel had a weakness for big ships and a passion for keeping up to date. The *Great Britain* showed clear marks of his personality. As though newfangled iron were not enough, Brunel gave her a displacement about twice as great as most of her competitors. She had the then unprecedented weight of 3,270 tons. Originally, Brunel had intended to drive the *Great Britain* with paddle wheels, but a new invention caused him to alter his thinking while his ship was being built.

The invention was the screw propeller, patented in 1836 by two separate workers, the Englishman Francis Smith and the Swede Captain John Ericsson. Smith started with clockwork models and progressed to a 6-ton launch, which he succeeded in driving with one of his water propellers. The result was so encouraging that in 1836 a much larger boat, the 240-ton *Archimedes*, was built and fitted with a Smith type of screw. In the meantime, Captain Ericsson had persuaded the U.S. Navy to order the screw-driven *Robert F. Stockton* from a Merseyside shipyard. Both vessels demonstrated the efficiency of the new mode of propulsion.

Brunel saw the *Archimedes* in Bristol Harbour in 1840 and was greatly impressed by her performance. Plans to drive the *Great Britain* by paddle wheels were dropped. She became not only the first big iron ship, but also the first really large vessel to be driven by a screw propeller. Her performance fulfilled all expectations. On her trials she achieved the very creditable speed of 11 knots and later proved the strength of iron beyond any doubt. In 1846 the *Great Britain* ran aground on the Irish coast. She took a battering from the sea that would have broken any wooden vessel, but when she was refloated eleven months later, her iron hull was still basically sound. After a refit, she was put on the Australia route on which she served for twenty-three years, with interruptions only for trooping duties during the Indian Mutiny in 1857, and the Crimean War. She was laid up in 1875 but reappeared in 1882 as an engineless sailing boat. Her sailing career ended in 1886, when she was damaged in a storm while trying to round the Horn. She reached the Falkland Islands, where she was relegated to use as a storage hulk. Her rusting but virtually indestructible hull was refloated in 1970 and towed back to England for renovation. The *Great Britain* proved the worth of iron, and big wooden ships became obsolete.

Not all passenger lines were eager to go over to screw propulsion, even after the *Great Britain*'s success. Cunard, for instance, did not make a general conversion to screw propulsion until 1862. The reason for this tardiness lay in an ancient tradition of the sea. Ever since Egyptian times the important passengers had been accommodated at the stern of the boat. Designers of early steam liners adhered faithfully to the old pattern. The first-class cabins were put in the traditional place of honour. This was satisfactory as long as the steamers were driven by paddles mounted near the centre of the boat. The staterooms were well away from noise and vibration. It was very different with a screw. The passengers who had paid most found themselves directly above the churning propeller. This was bad enough when the weather was fair, but when it was foul and a racing screw came clear of the water, it was unbearable. Moneyed people complained and tended to patronize paddle steamers. It was only after the position of the first-class cabins had been altered that screw-driven liners came into their own and banished paddle boats from the Atlantic.

The most memorable of all mid-nineteenth-century liners was Brunel's gigantic *Great Eastern*, which was under construction at Millwall on the Thames from 1854 to 1857. Her overall length of 692 feet and her loaded displacement of 32,000 tons dwarfed anything else afloat. She was by far the largest ship of her day. Her length was not surpassed until the White Star liner *Oceanic* was launched in 1899. The *Great Eastern* had two sets of engines, one driving a screw and the other paddle wheels. Just to be on the safe side, she also carried six masts with a good spread of canvas. Smoke from the coal-fired boilers escaped through no fewer than five funnels, so that the great ship looked something like a floating factory decorated with sails.

Even before she was afloat, the *Great Eastern* proved to be an unlucky ship. Disputes and quarrels delayed her building, and the shipyard where she lay went bankrupt and was seized by creditors. Brunel's company had to pay a heavy rent to the owners of the yard and was forced to launch her before preparations had been thoroughly tested. The company faced a difficult task. The 12,000-ton bulk of the iron hull was the greatest weight that anyone had ever tried to shift. Furthermore, the ship was to be pushed gently sideways into the water and not allowed to career into the narrow river down a slipway. The launch was originally attempted in November, 1857, but the huge ship stuck fast. Three months of persuasion by batteries of hydraulic rams were needed to nudge her into the water. The efforts to get the *Great Eastern* floated broke Brunel's health and the owners' finances. A new company was soon formed, but the great designer never lived to see his creation cross the Atlantic. There was an explosion on the *Great Eastern* as she steamed down the English Channel on her trials. News reached Brunel on his sickbed, and the disappointment was too great for him. He died shortly afterward.

The *Great Eastern* never prospered as a passenger ship. There was too much

The Great Eastern *in New York Harbour, 1860. She was a triumph of engineering and by far the largest ship of her day, but she never prospered as a passenger liner.*

competition on the North Atlantic for her to attract enough passengers to fill her giant hull. Her fuel consumption was enormous, and although her performance was no disgrace for her day, she never got within about 6 mph of her designed speed of 20 knots.

After only a few years of service, she was auctioned for a mere £25,000. Her new owners chartered her for cable laying, and the *Great Eastern* found her niche. In 1886 she was used for the laying of the first successful transatlantic cable. Other similar jobs followed. On one occasion she left England bound for Bombay via the Cape of Good Hope, so loaded down by the cable to be laid that she displaced the amazing total of 32,724 tons. She was undoubtedly the leviathan of her day.

Steam had made the gigantic *Great Eastern* possible, but it had not quite driven sails from the sea. Engines still consumed a tremendous amount of fuel, and coaling stations had to be set up before steamers could venture into distant parts of the globe. These preparations were very costly and made many owners favour sailing ships for long voyages. Warships could not afford to be too reliant on coal supplies either. Often, patrols visited isolated waters where no fueling facilities existed. Until quite late in the century, warships had sails, as well as engines, and the order "Hoist screw, set sails" was common on all naval vessels. However, despite objections from traditionalists, no warship powered by sails alone was built after about 1850.

The opening of the Suez Canal in 1869 proved a severe blow to sailing interests. It shortened both the route to the East and the distance between coaling stations. Steamers needed less fuel and had more room left for cargo. Even the beautiful and speedy tea clippers found the voyage to China uneconomical and were diverted by their owners into the Australian wool trade, where some, like the *Cutty Sark* and *Thermopylae*, acquired great reputations.

As more and more parts of the world came within their reach, steamers continued to develop and improve. However, striking improvements were sometimes slow to catch on. Early screw-driven ships had only one propeller. 91

If this were damaged, a ship had to rely on its sails to take it out of trouble. An obvious safety measure was to provide two screws working on separate shafts. The first full-size twin-screw steamer was the 400-ton *Flora*, which was built on the Thames in 1862. Other small ships followed her example, but twenty-six years elapsed before the first giant twin-screwer, the *City of Paris*, appeared on the Atlantic in 1888. By then the advantages of multiple propellers were clear. If one screw were disabled, the other could still drive the ship, while, in the event of rudder damage, the vessel could be steered by running the propellers at different speeds. Some designers, however, continued to put their faith in auxiliary sails and kept to single screws. It was only during the 1890's that public uneasiness forced the general adoption of multiple propellers for all big ships. Auxiliary sails were then no longer needed, and they quickly disappeared from the scene.

The first metal ships were made of iron. Steel was a stronger material, but more expensive. It was used only initially, when both strength and lightness of construction were needed. The first steel ship to cross the Atlantic was the 325-ton *Banshee*, a fast paddle steamer made in Liverpool in 1862. She was intended as a blockade-runner in the American Civil War, and steel was chosen to reduce her weight so that she could be as speedy as possible. Ordinary ships were made of iron until the late 1870's, when new methods were devised to mass produce steel and lower its cost. Large steel ships then became a commercial possibility. The first sizeable vessel to make use of the opportunity was the 4,000-ton *Buenos Ayrean* of 1879, which plied between Britain and Canada. Cunard's first steel ship, the *Servia*, made her maiden voyage in 1881. She also had the distinction of being the first ship to be electrically lighted.

The nineteenth century had certainly witnessed some remarkable changes at sea: steel, steam, and electric light in place of wood, sail, and the hurricane lamp. It did not seem possible that anything more could happen, but it did.

Sir Charles Parsons was dissatisfied with conventional steam engines. The up-and-down movement of their pistons had to be changed somehow into the rotation needed to drive the propellers. It would be more efficient, he argued, to use steam power to produce circular motion to start with. In 1884 Sir Charles made a turbine in which high-pressure steam was squirted against blades set around the rims of a series of wheels mounted on the same axle. The wheels were sent spinning at great speed. Parsons had the circular motion he required. The new type of engine had plenty of teething troubles. Often the wheels, or rotors, as they were called, flew to pieces as the turbine worked up to full power.

Eventually Parsons overcame all the difficulties. By 1894 a turbine was

H.M.S. Nile, *a screw-and-sail warship of the British Navy, 1855.*

ready to be fitted into a specially built ship, the long, slim *Turbinia*, which displaced $44\frac{1}{2}$ tons. Sir Charles received little official encouragement in his efforts but caused a sensation when he gate-crashed the 1897 naval review with his little turbine craft. The uninvited guest dashed among the assembled warships at the unheard-of speed of $34\frac{1}{2}$ knots. The British Admiralty could not ignore this performance, and two turbine-driven destroyers were ordered for the service. They were the first of a long line. Today every major vessel uses turbine engines.

The Servia, *the Cunard Company's first steel-built liner, made her maiden voyage in 1881.*

The Turbinia, *the first turbine driven ship, dashed among the warships assembled for the Royal Navy's 1897 review at the unheard-of speed of more than thirty-four knots.*

8

The Nineteenth Century: 3
Developments in the Air

Balloons were a reality before the nineteenth century dawned, and controlled airship flight was achieved by the time the century was halfway over. These were advances that ordinary men could understand and accept. Balloons and airships were lighter than air and floated upward naturally. Heavier-than-air flight, on the other hand, seemed far less feasible. Those who experimented with wings got little public applause and a great deal of scorn. Eminent scientists condemned their efforts as futile. Despite this, the world was brought to the very edge of powered aeroplane flight by the time the century ended.

The initiator of this progress, was the scholarly Yorkshire gentleman Sir George Cayley. At the end of the eighteenth century he had realized that one set of wings could not supply both lift and propulsion. From then on, his plan was to have fixed wings to provide lift with entirely separate paddles, or propellers, to push the aircraft forward. He had made a complete break with the age of wing flappers.

The first decade of the nineteenth century was one of the most productive of Cayley's life. He theorized, experimented, flew models, and even made a full-size aircraft. In 1804 he built a whirling arm device, which swept a model wing through the air at a high speed. The wing was inclined at different angles so that he could study how much weight it would lift in each position. Cayley lost no time in applying the knowledge gained from this experiment. He constructed a model which became the prototype for all later aeroplanes. This historic model was simplicity itself. Its body was a plain wooden pole, while its wings were an ordinary kite fixed to the fuselage at an angle of six degrees. The tail, which had a horizontal surface and a vertical fin, was attached to the main part of the body by a universal joint that could be swivelled in any direction. Cayley wrote of his model that "it was very pretty to see it sail down a steep hill" and of its control that "the least inclination of the tail towards the right or left made it shape its course like a ship by the rudder."

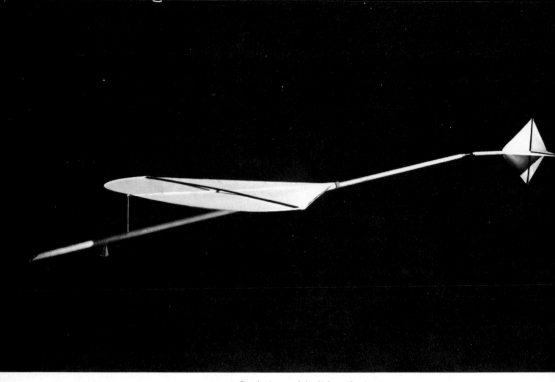

Cayley's model glider of 1804.

Other experiments followed. Streamlining was investigated, the lift of curved, or cambered, wings was measured, and a way of giving an aeroplane stability by angling its wings upward was discovered. All this work culminated in the full-size glider of 1809, which had a wing area of about 300 square feet.

Cayley's successes with models and the glider made him ambitious for powered flight. He had the flying machine; all he needed was an engine to drive it into the air. Steam engines were out of the question. They were much too heavy and cumbersome. A new type of motor was required, and Sir George tried hard to design one. His hot-air engine and a strange device using small charges of gunpowder did work after a fashion, but not well enough for an aeroplane. Powered aircraft would have to wait for another age.

Frustrated in his attempts to make an aeroplane engine, Cayley turned his attentions to balloons, which he realized were useless as practical vehicles as long as they were at the mercy of the wind. Sir George was one of the first to make sensible suggestions for turning the balloon into a dirigible, or steerable, airship, which would go in the direction its pilot required. He published several useful papers on this topic during 1816–17, but for many years afterward allowed his talents to lie dormant. His energy was so taken up by rearing his family of ten children and by politics that little was left for aeronautical research.

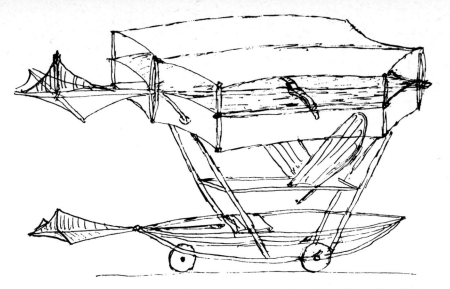

Cayley's boy-carrying glider of 1849. From a sketch made by Cayley himself.

Cayley's old interests eventually reasserted themselves. In 1843 he conceived one of his most original and ambitious designs. It was for a convertiplane, which was to take off vertically before proceeding into forward flight. Four wide-bladed helicopter rotors were to give initial lift and then close up to make circular wing surfaces. The forward thrust was to come from two pusher propellers at the rear of the machine. Present-day aviation is still struggling with the problems of vertical takeoff, so it is not surprising that Cayley's project got no further than the plans.

By the late 1840's Sir George was an old man, but his interest in aeronautics was unabated. In 1849 he made a full-size triplane glider. This was normally flown loaded with ballast, but on one occasion it had a human passenger. A note in Cayley's handwriting records that a ten-year-old boy was floated downhill on the glider for a short flight.

Sir George Cayley's importance in the history of flight is hard to over-emphasize. It was he who was the first to realize that a plane surface inclined to a flow of air would give lift. It was he again who was the first to notice that a cambered surface would give more lift than a flat one. He was the first man to learn how to control an aircraft and the first to use positive dihedral, or upward-sloping, wings to give stability to a glider. These and other achievements would make him important enough in themselves, but in addition to this, his works were widely read and influenced nearly every major pioneer up to the time of the Wright brothers.

Two of the great Yorkshireman's earliest disciples were William Henson and John Stringfellow, who both lived at Chard in Somerset. Henson was the first of the pair to become intrigued by Cayley's writings. He began experiments of his own and in 1843 produced plans for a monoplane of mammoth proportions. Its huge cambered wing stretched for 150

97

Henson's ambitious Aerial Steam Carriage design of 1843.

feet and carried beneath it a fuselage big enough to hold a steam engine and the crew. Driving bands led from the motor to two six-bladed propellers fixed just aft of the wing. A short boom reached back from the crew's cabin and supported a tail plane and a vertical rudder. The tail plane included an elevator, which could make the machine climb or dive. The whole design looked surprisingly modern. It had only one major fault. Henson, despite Cayley's discoveries, gave no dihedral angle to the wings. If his aircraft had tilted in flight, it would not have been able to right itself automatically.

Henson was not satisfied with plans alone. He wanted to build an actual aircraft. His friend, Stringfellow, was brought in to design a special light engine, and an attempt was made to raise funds for the construction of a full-size aerial steam carriage. Imaginative prints were issued showing the plane as though it were a reality, sailing majestically over the roofs of London and Paris. These pictures made Henson's design famous, but they brought in no money. The aerial steamer stayed firmly on the drawing board.

Henson's next step was to enlist Stringfellow's help in building a steam-

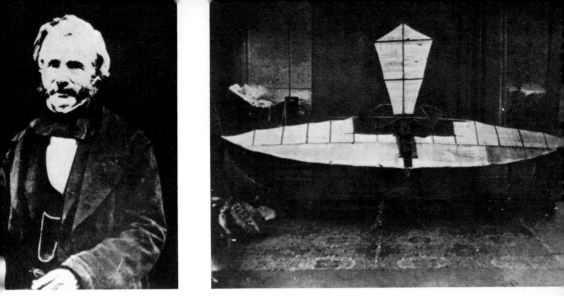

Stringfellow and his powered aircraft of 1848.

powered model of his larger design. The model was itself a sizable thing and had a wingspan of 20 feet. No doubt, the inventors hoped it would prove the worth of a full-size aircraft. Unfortunately, it did nothing of the sort. When it was launched in 1847 on Bala Down near Chard, it could manage only a clumsy downhill flight. Henson was disappointed and went off to make his fortune in America.

By this time, however, Stringfellow's enthusiasm was roused. He decided to carry on experiments by himself. In 1848 he made another model with the smaller wingspan of 10 feet. It was powered like its predecessor, with a miniature steam engine of Stringfellow's own design. Until recently it was believed that this small model made successful indoor flights in both Chard and London, but now some doubts have been cast on these claims. Whatever their success may have been, the two Henson-Stringfellow models were certainly the earliest powered aeroplanes and have an assured place in aeronautical history for this reason alone.

After Henson and Stringfellow, powered heavier-than-air flight still seemed as far away as ever, but already great strides had been taken in the development of the airship. Ever since the first ascent, ways had been sought to free the balloon from the mercy of the wind. Ideas ranged from pushing the balloons along with futile, feathered paddles to the utterly madcap scheme of towing them along with teams of trained eagles. Men like Cayley brought some common sense to bear on the problem. During the first few decades of the nineteenth century it was realized that navigable balloons would have to be streamlined and driven by engine operated screw propellers. The 1840's saw several model airships. Some were driven by small steam engines, but one made in 1843 by the Englishman Monck Mason had a clockwork motor.

The first full-size powered airship was flown by the French engineer Henri Giffard in 1852. Buoyancy came from a 143-foot long sausage-shaped balloon, which was filled with coal gas. Beneath and well clear of this envelope hung a long wooden beam from which was in turn suspended a platform for the pilot and a steam engine. Giffard very wisely kept as much distance as possible between the boiler of his engine and the highly inflammable coal gas in the envelope above. The 3-hp engine was used to drive an airscrew 11 feet in diameter.

Giffard, wearing a top hat, embarked on the inaugural flight from Paris. The engine was started up, ropes were cast off, and the airship chugged away on its 17-mile journey to Trappes at a steady 6 mph. The low speed suited

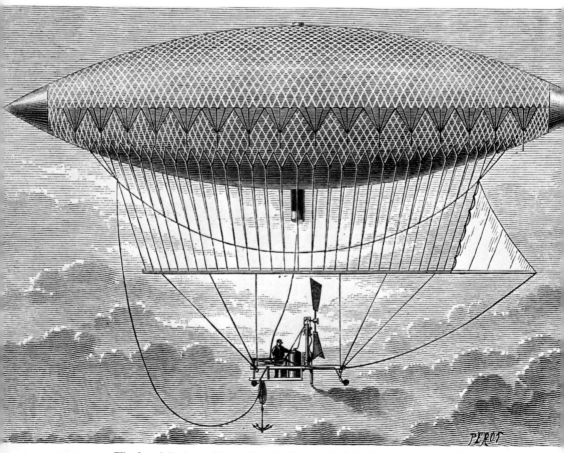

The first full-size, self-propelled airship was built by the Frenchman Giffard in 1852.

the inventor's headgear, but did not give the large, sail-like rudder enough grip on the air to steer the machine properly. Giffard's airship was a great step forward but was not a complete success.

Next, the engineer tried to make a faster craft that would be easier to steer. In 1855 he completed a new airship with a much slimmer envelope than its predecessor. Unfortunately, the gasbag burst during its first test flight. Giffard escaped the crash with his life but lost all further enthusiasm for airship design.

Haelein's airship of 1872 raised the speed record to 10 mph, but this German inventor used gas from the envelope as fuel for the engine. The farther the machine flew, the less buoyant it became, so that it can hardly rank as a practicable device.

The first really feasible airship was the *La France*, built in 1884 by the two Frenchmen Renard and Kreps. Its 8 hp electric motor was driven by special lightweight batteries and, for the first time, gave an airship enough power to return to its starting point even against an adverse wind. In still air the aircraft could manage a speed of about 14 mph. The envelope was a stream-lined hydrogen balloon some 165 feet long.

Airships came into their own in the late 1890's when light but powerful petrol engines became readily available. The first airship to employ a petrol engine was built by the German Schwarz in 1897. Another new idea was also tried out on the same machine. Instead of using a soft envelope which inflated like a toy balloon when gas was blown in, Schwarz made a rigid framework of aluminium girders into which the gasbags fitted. The aircraft failed, but in 1898 another German, Count von Zeppelin, began work on a design with a similar rigid skeleton. It was finished in 1900 and was not totally effective, but from it were evolved a race of giant Zeppelin airships which were used for bombing and became one of the most feared weapons of the World War I.

Despite the advance of airships, many inventors persevered with the aeroplane. During the middle years of the nineteenth century the centre of such activities shifted from England to France.

Perhaps the most important of the early French pioneers of the aeroplane was the naval officer Félix Du Temple. He was a man of scientific disposition and studied Cayley's works, verifying what he read by flying powered model aircraft. One of his models was the first machine in history to rise from the ground under its own power and complete a flight without mishap. In 1857, at about the time he was experimenting with models, Du Temple designed a full-size aircraft. It was a monoplane, whose cambered, fabric-covered wings had enough dihedral to stop the machine from tilting sideways in

Left: Du Temple's piloted steam aircraft of 1874, though a brave attempt, was unable to sustain itself in flight.

Right: A model of the Frenchman Ader's Eole of 1890. The fabric has been removed from one wing to show the construction. This steam-driven machine achieved short hopping flights, but the pilot was a mere passenger with no control over the aircraft's movements.

flight. At the rear of the short body was a tail plane and a vertical rudder. The aircraft was to be driven by a propeller at the nose. Du Temple could find no really suitable engine but toyed with the idea of either steam or electricity. After a long delay, he settled on steam and actually built a man-carrying machine. In about 1874 it was ready for testing and was launched down a sloping ramp with a sailor at the controls. The steam engine did not give enough power, and the aircraft made only a short, descending flight.

Another Frenchman was Clément Ader, who in 1889 built the *Eole*, a batlike aircraft with a 46-foot wingspan. Ader ignored most of what was already known about wing design, control, and stability and concentrated his hopes on a really powerful steam engine. The machine was tested in 1890 and careered over the ground so quickly that it did take off and stay airborne for a few yards. It cannot be claimed that the *Eole* flew, since Ader was simply a passenger with no control at all over his aircraft. It would be better to say that it hopped.

The French Army became interested and contributed money for further tests. The second machine that Ader had wanted to build was never completed, but a third, *Avion*, was ready in 1897. The *Avion* never managed to leave the ground for as much as a yard. Its only achievement was to give the French their word for an aeroplane.

Not all the pioneers of these years were French, of course. One was a Russian, Mozhaiski, whose aircraft achieved a powered flight in 1884, after it had been launched down a sloping ramp. The machine was a steam-driven monoplane, which was propelled by both tractor and pusher airscrews. Great claims are sometimes made for this aeroplane, but the truth is that even after it had hurtled down a "ski jump", its pilot, Golubev, could only persuade it to make a short, staggering flight.

All the pioneers of the late nineteenth century were overshadowed by one man, the German Otto Lilienthal (1848–96). Even as a boy, Lilienthal was enthralled by the idea of flight and had once made a set of flapping wings, which he had tested at night to avoid ridicule. When he grew up, he became

Lilienthal, the great German pioneer, flying in one of his gliders, 1896.

an engineer, but his spare time was always devoted to aeronautics. To learn more, he studied the flight of birds and became such an expert that he wrote a book on the subject.

By 1891 he was ready to put his accumulated knowledge to work and built the first of a series of gliders. The wings fitted around the pilot and were light enough for him to run forward and launch himself into the air by a final jump onto a springboard. Later, Lilienthal went out to hills near Berlin and just ran down an incline until the glider gathered sufficient speed to become airborne. In 1892 he made his own artificial mound and, from this, made many glides of 100 yards or more, with his sequence of graceful, bird-like aeroplanes. His gliders were mostly monoplanes, but he experimented with bi-planes as well. Both types had fixed tail planes and fins, and, with one exception, the pilot, who hung by his elbows and shoulders from a frame at the centre of the wings, controlled his machine by slightly shifting the weight of his body. The exception was Lilienthal's last glider. On this, a thong around the pilot's forehead led back to an elevator at the rear. By nodding his head, Lilienthal could raise or lower the elevator and make the machine climb or dive.

All these gliders were leading up to the final objective—powered flight. In 1896 Lilienthal came near this with a new machine. It was similar to the gliders except for flapping wingtips driven by compressed carbon dioxide gas. The inventor never lived to test it, however. On August 9, 1896, Lilienthal was making a routine flight on the glider which he had modified with an elevator. He seemed to be performing as expertly as usual, but suddenly the wind dropped. For a moment the pilot was confused and moved his head in the wrong direction. Before he could recover the machine fell out of control and smashed into the ground. Lilienthal broke his spine and died the next day. His last words are said to have been, "Sacrifices must be made."

The flights of the great German pioneer were world-famous, and he was the direct inspiration of the Wright brothers. After his death they decided to take up where he had left off. What they achieved in the twentieth century, the whole world knows.

9

The Rise of the Motor-car

Technically, man has progressed further in the twentieth century than he did in the previous million years of his existence. Changes have been outstanding. When the century opened, the Western nations were justly proud of their efficient railways and steamships, but the car was still the rich man's toy. Properly controlled flight seemed a dream of the very distant future, and space travel utter fantasy.

In 1900 the car was an open vehicle, notorious for its unreliability and lack of comfort. Passengers cowered inside their protective clothing as their mounts lurched over potholes or swayed around the awkward bends of the inadequate roads. In winter, car owners froze, and, in summer, they choked in clouds of dust thrown up from the loose road surfaces. The public and the police forces were largely hostile to these noisy intruders. The early motorist had to be dedicated.

Cars, with their engine-driven wheels, put an unlooked for strain on roads which had been designed for freerolling horse-drawn traffic. Both braking and acceleration tended to tear up the road surface, and things were not helped by the steel strips which were set into car tyres to stop them from skidding. Most countries imposed speed restrictions as much to save their roads as from any desire for safety.

Fortunately, an alternative to the loose macadam method of road making had been invented in the 1880's by the Frenchman Girardeau and the Italian Rimini. After sweeping and rolling, men with cans of liquid tar sprayed the surface. A sprinkling of sand finished the process, and after a few days, a dust-free road was open to traffic.

During these early pioneering days of motoring, Continental designs were supreme, and the monarch of them all was the German Mercedes, which had been developed from Daimler's earlier cars. By 1903 the British Napier was beginning to challenge the German lead, but it was not until 1907 that the partnership of C. S. Rolls and Sir Henry Royce produced a vehicle which finally outclassed the Mercedes. The 1907 Rolls-Royce, the *Silver*

The original Rolls-Royce Silver Ghost. This car was built in 1907, and after 500,000 miles of motoring, is still in good running order.

Ghost stayed in production virtually unchanged until after World War I and maintained its superb quality despite the death of Rolls in a flying accident in 1910.

While Europe was still concentrating on high quality and individual workmanship, the United States was beginning to put the emphasis on quantity of production. Cars were turned out in ever-increasing numbers at prices which ordinary people could afford. Standard models with interchangeable spare parts also ensured speedy and effective repairs.

Henry Ford was the great exponent of mass production, and his genius for organization made motoring possible for the millions. His was the first motor factory built around an assembly line. It was one-fifth of a mile long and poured out cars at a rate undreamed of in Europe until the 1930's. Between 1908 and 1927, 15,000,000 Ford Model T's or Tin Lizzies, as they were affectionately called, left his workshops. Today the Model T may look quaint, but it, more than any other vehicle, made the United States car-conscious. Just prior to the First World War the United States was producing more than four times as many cars as the whole of Europe.

With the car came the quest for speed. Racing cars appeared and did much to help in the development of more reliable engines for everyday use. Performances soared, and records were established and broken on race-tracks, like the one at Brooklands in Surrey. Brooklands saw many memorable events, but two were outstanding. First, there was Edge's 24-hour drive in a Napier during 1907, when he averaged 65 mph, and then there was Percy Lambert's epic drive in a streamlined Talbot in 1912, which made him the first man to cover 100 miles in an hour.

Little time remained before Europe was to be caught up in an all-consuming war. In 1913 William Morris made his first motor-car, the famous bull-nosed Morris Oxford, but in the next year the storm which had been threatening for so long broke. Cars were turned to warlike purposes. It was no longer gay young ladies who rode in elegant motor-cars, but grim-faced staff officers on their way to conferences. The fighting troops made do with humbler vehicles. Ex-civilian trucks or even early buses were good enough to carry them to the slaughter. Design tended to stagnate, but it was perhaps

The Ford Model T, popularly known as Tin Lizzie. Fifteen million were produced between 1908 and 1927.

World War I, more than anything else, which convinced people that the car was here to stay. Railways, with their fixed tracks, were soon shown to be vulnerable to war damage, while motor vehicles could drive around shell holes, cross emergency pontoon bridges, and make their way right up to the forward positions. The generals were impressed. The war effort made use of more vehicles during its four years than the whole world had possessed in 1914. The motor vehicle had proved its worth and won its place in society.

The war produced one completely new land weapon, the heavily armoured tank. Colonel, later General, Sir Ernest Swinton got the idea from watching American Holt caterpillar tractors towing guns behind the lines. The War Office would give no firm support, but the suggestion was taken up enthusiastically by Winston Churchill, who was then First Lord of the Admiralty. A simple ruse was used to bring the new weapon under the Admiralty's jurisdiction. It was simply called a landship, and to this day, nautical terms, like turret and hull (for the body), are used to describe its parts. For secrecy, the hull and chassis were made in different places, and the hull was labelled as a water carrier for Mesopotamia. The workmen called the hull "that tank thing," and the name has stuck and been incorporated into many languages. Tanks took the enemy by surprise and, if properly used, might well have broken the stalemate of trench warfare. The generals, however, still preferred their cavalry, and it was not until the Second World War that tanks really showed their potential.

After the disruptions of the war, it took some time for the motor industry to settle down to peacetime conditions. The cars of 1914 had already begun to lose the top-heavy look of their predecessors. They were reasonably reliable, and although they were usually open, the passengers were at least protected by windshields and hoods. Electric starters had begun to appear, and acetylene lamps were gradually being replaced by electric bulbs. In the first few postwar years, most manufacturers were content to follow up these general tendencies, rather than to start immediately on completely new models.

One of the earliest of the new generation of cars was the Hispano-Suiza of 1919. This was a particularly fine machine with a motor developed from an aeroplane engine and with braking on all four wheels. The latter feature was not unique, but it was certainly unusual on a car of that period. It was not until the mid-1920's that the increasing number of road accidents forced all producers to install four-wheel braking on their vehicles.

The 1920's saw the real blossoming of the motor industry. Cheap family models appeared, and the age of the Sunday drive began. More and more private cars made their way onto the roads and jostled with the

The first tank was the British Mark 1, which saw service in World War I.

surplus army trucks that had flooded the market when the First World War ended. These trucks did not take long to prove themselves more convenient carriers of goods than railways for short hauls, and soon more were crowding onto the inadequate highways. By 1925 the United States had 2,000,000 commercial vehicles, France had some 250,000 and Britain more than 200,000. None of the roads had been built to take this volume of traffic, and casualties mounted alarmingly. It became clear that new and redesigned roads were required.

The stock market crash of 1929 and the subsequent Depression threw millions out of work, and road improvement and building programmes were used to provide employment. In both Europe and the United States, thousands of miles of roads were built by the armies of the unemployed.

Germany led the way with her *Autobahnen*, which, like the earlier Italian *autostrade*, were reserved for motor vehicles alone. The first intercity *Autobahn* was begun in 1929 and linked Cologne and Bonn. The road was carried over other roads, a railway, and a town suburb. But one disastrous error was made—no space was left between opposing traffic lanes. Many head-on crashes occurred between cars travelling in the fast lanes, and fatalities were frequent.

This mistake was not repeated when the full *Autobahn* programme was enthusiastically launched by the Nazis on their coming to power in 1933. Hitler

The Austin 7 of 1922 was the first four-seater "baby" car. It made motoring possible for many ordinary Britons.

Opposite: The Austin A.40 of 1947, one of the new breed of European cars designed immediately after World War II.

The Buick Sedan of 1925, a typical American motor-car of its period.

saw the building of roads as a means of bolstering German prestige, decreasing the unemployment problem, and speeding troop movements. Under his regime, 2,500 miles of dual-carriage roadway were constructed.

Similar roads were being built in the United States. The new highways passed over or under existing roads and stretched majestically over the

countryside. Curves were gentle, gradients were easy, and traffic could enter or leave only at carefully designed junctions. Everything was done to ensure maximum safety combined with the highest possible speed.

Although the Depression did not slow down road building, it proved disastrous for many of the smaller car manufacturers. Until then, cars had been built in Europe by the old coachbuilding technique. Metal panels were attached by hand to a wooden-framed bodywork, and the interior of the vehicle was carefully upholstered. It was a job for craftsmen and cost money.

When the slump came, only the larger motor firms could afford to stay in business, and even they were forced to alter their ways. New mass production methods were imported into Europe from the United States. Cars were no longer made by hand. Body sections were stamped out of sheet steel by huge machines and passed along a production line to be welded together. Costs were reduced, but, at first, quality suffered.

It was not until after the gap caused by the Second World War that the European car manufacturers finally mastered mass production techniques. The cars of the late 1940's looked better, lasted longer, and were easier to drive than their prewar predecessors. A good example was the British Austin A.40 of 1947.

Automatic transmission was introduced in the late 1930's by the American Oldsmobile Company. Although initially viewed with suspicion this technical advance has gradually won favour, until today some 75 per cent of new American cars have dispensed with manual gear changing.

The first turbine-powered car was this experimental Rover of 1950.

The 1968 Buick Electra. A modern American automobile with automatic transmission.

It is possible that cars of the future will be gas-turbine-powered and achieve gear-free driving without the expense of a complicated automatic transmission system. The world's first turbine car was made by the British Rover Company in 1950. It set the first speed record for its class in 1953, when it was driven at 151 mph along a motorway in Belgium. Several other experimental turbine cars have appeared since then, but perhaps the most successful has been the Rover/BRM. This proved its reliability by lasting the course for the whole of the 1963 Le Mans Twenty-four-hour race. However, the problem of disposing of the hot exhaust gases has not been solved, and no turbine car is yet on the commercial market.

In the last few years, several motor manufacturers have been experimenting with electric cars. Electric traction has many advantages. It is silent, fume-free, needs little maintenance, and, like the turbine, eliminates gear shifting. The only drawback is the weight and size of the electrical storage batteries that have to be carried around. Recent research offers the hope that lighter, less cumbersome batteries will be evolved and thus open the way for small, silent-running town cars, which could be recharged at night by plugging them into the electrical mains. Families of the future may well own an electric runabout for city use and a powerful turbine car for long-distance driving.

The Austin Mini, a modern successor to the Austin 7 of the 1920's.

The line started by Daimler's motorcycle of 1885 still continues. The photograph shows a powerful modern motorcycle made by Norton, one of the most famous British manufacturers.

An experimental electric car built by the Ford M. Company.

10

The Twentieth Century:
Railways, Changes at Sea

All the major industrial countries entered the twentieth century with efficient railways operated by powerful steam locomotives. Here and there, electric power had been used, but to the man in the street, it would have seemed inconceivable that within about fifty years steam would have almost disappeared from the railways of advanced nations.

Italy was the first country to electrify main lines on anything like a large scale. Her system, which worked on 3,000 volts, was started in 1902. More sensational, but less important in the long run, was a German achievement of the same year, when an electric locomotive reached the amazing speed of 130·4 mph on an experimental line near Berlin. It was probably the example of the successful Italian practice, as well as her own abundant supplies of cheap electricity from hydroelectric schemes, which made Switzerland decide to go in for a massive electrification of her railway lines toward the end of World War I.

During the interwar years most European countries tested electric traction on at least some stretches of line. Nearly everywhere, overhead conductors were used, and the British Southern Railway was alone in using a third rail to carry the current. Steam power was still predominant, but it was not without rivals.

The devastation caused by World War II meant that many European railways had to embark on massive rebuilding schemes. This was both a burden and an opportunity. New systems could be adopted; electricity could be given its big chance. There was much to commend it. Electric locomotives are comparatively simple and easy to maintain. They can generate immense power as they start off, exactly what is needed to give a train a quick getaway. Electric motors give off no unpleasant or harmful fumes. In fact, there is only one serious drawback, and that is the initial cost of fitting all the current-carrying conductors. A line has to be used intensively to make this outlay a paying proposition. Once in operation, however, electric trains are smooth-running, silent, clean and fast. French electric locomotives exceeded 200 mph in trials held in 1955, and trains on the new Tokaido line in Japan cruise at speeds of about 125 mph. To many people, electricity seems to be the power for the trains of the future.

The world's fastest train. An electric express on Japan's New Tokaido Line passing through Tokyo.

At present, electricity has a competitor in the diesel engine. The first big diesel locomotive was built by the German company of Diesel-Klose-Sulzer in 1912. It had a 1,000 hp engine but was used only for test purposes. A much humbler Swedish diesel-electric of 1913 was the first to see regular service. It had a diesel engine of only 75 hp, but this was used to drive a generator, which supplied electricity to an electric driving motor. In this way, the difficulty of supplying the diesel's power to the wheels was very cunningly overcome without the need for an elaborate gearbox.

During the 1920's there were occasional experiments with diesels. Some, like the American Locomotive Company's diesel-electric shunting engine,

*German two-car diesel-electric trains of the
1930's could top 100 mph.*

which stayed in service from 1925 until 1957, were great successes, but most were failures. Major developments had to wait till the 1930's.

It was Germany, the birthplace of diesel engines, which was most successful in pioneering their use in locomotives. In 1932 the Germans started a two-car diesel-electric train service between Berlin and Hamburg. Although the combined power of its two motors gave only 800 hp, the train often topped 100 mph, and averaged 77.4 mph over the whole 160-mile journey. 117

This Hawker Siddeley 4,000 hp diesel-electric prototype was sold in 1971 to the U.S.S.R. for testing on Soviet railways.

Similar express services spread across Germany. Diesels became a prestige symbol, and many European countries began to follow the German lead. The United States, too, took up the diesel and produced her first main-line diesel-electric locomotive, the *Pioneer Zephyr*, in 1934. This was an immediate success and stayed in use for twenty-five years.

Britain, however, clung to her well-tried steam locomotives, which in the 1930's could still compete on even terms with any train in the world. With war again looming in the background, it did not seem wise to make the country even more reliant on oil from abroad. Steam trains had the great advantage of burning home-produced coal.

After World War II the gradual swing to main-line diesels begun in the 1930's was speeded up, and even Britain began to discard her cherished steam engines. Now, in the 1970's, the change to diesel and electric power is almost complete in the Western world, and the few steam locomotives 118 to escape the scrap-yards have been relegated to museums.

Not only have railways had to cope with new equipment, but conditions have also changed, and competition for passengers and freight has become fiercer. Once the railways had it all their own way, but motor transport and aircraft have completely altered the situation. Motor vehicles are more flexible and economical for short freighting journeys. They can deliver right to the door. Long-distance passengers are attracted by the sheer speed of aircraft. For distances of less than 100 miles, road transportation is superior to rail, while, for distances of more than 200 miles, aircraft are presenting a distinct challenge.

All railways seem to lose money on commuter services. Rush-hour traffic takes up more track and rolling stock than is justified by off-peak demand. However, if the great cities are not to be strangled by their own road traffic, it is essential that their rail services should not be diminished. Several American cities have, in fact, taken a step in the opposite direction and begun to increase their suburban train coverage. In the San Francisco area alone, a new 75-mile network of track was brought into service in 1972.

European cities have largely favoured extending old or building new underground railways. Paris, Milan, Rotterdam, Madrid, Munich, Frankfurt and Stockholm all have started new underground lines in the last few years. Even London, with its already impressive mileage for Underground trains found it necessary to add the Victoria Line, part of which was opened in 1968.

After nine years of experiment France abandoned its air-cushion monorail in 1974.

Another suggested method of lessening road traffic is the extensive use of monorails. The single rail is usually supported well clear of the ground, and trains may be either suspended below it or balanced to run above it. A public line from the center of Tokyo to the airport was opened in the early 1960's; another was built in Seattle. In France research was initiated in 1965 on an air-cushion monorail system, but despite the attainment of speeds of 190 mph the project was abandoned in 1974 in favour of conventional high-speed trains. Monorail tracks are comparatively cheap to put up and may be suspended over roads or railways, causing little disturbance to existing buildings. However, there are disadvantages. If a train breaks down between stations, it is difficult to extricate the passengers, while it is also quite tricky to arrange junctions between different tracks. A further drawback is the decreased stability compared with that of a conventional train. This means that the passengers get a less comfortable ride. After an exhaustive study, the authorities in charge of the great San Francisco Bay railway extension decided to use only ordinary trains. Their decision must be respected as based on sound judgment. If monorails have a place in the future, it is probably in providing a specialized service, such as a fast line to an airport, rather than a complete commuter network.

Railways have been forced out of their old habits by the success of the motor vehicle, but cars and trucks have been almost too successful for their own good. Their numbers have multiplied to the point where road-crowding in the cities provides one of the major justifications for the continuance of urban train services. In long-distance passenger travel and in freighting operations, the railways have altered their methods and seem to have a reduced, but still considerable, part to play in the economic lives of the nations. Railways are not yet ready to disappear from the scene.

The first decade of the century was taken up largely by maritime rivalry between Britain and Germany. Huge ironclad warships thundered down the slipways by the score, and all the engineering skill that each nation could muster was used to make its warships and liners mistresses of the seas.

Soon the new turbine engines that had been developed at the turn of the century were to be embroiled in the struggle, but first they were put to humbler uses. The first turbine merchantman was the insignificant little *King Edward* of 1901, which was a river steamer on the Clyde. Three years later, the first sizeable turbine liners, the 10,750-ton Allan Line *Virginian* and *Victorian*, made an appearance. These vessels could reach 20 knots, but like their smaller predecessors, they had to overcome numerous mechanical teething troubles. Despite these difficulties, turbines were catching on, and

The Carmania, *the Cunard Company's first turbine ship.*

The ill-fated Titanic *took 1,503 passengers and crew with her to a watery grave after colliding with an iceberg on her maiden voyage in 1912.*

as more entered service, their superiority over conventional steam engines was becoming more obvious.

In 1905 Cunard built two 19,500-ton ships, very similar except for the types of engine installed. Here was to be the crucial test. The *Caronia* was to be powered by reciprocating steam engines, while the *Carmania* was to be fitted with turbines. There could be no doubt which was the better ship. The *Carmania* was three-quarters of a knot faster and still more economical to run than her sister ship.

This experiment decided the influential Cunard Line to use turbines in their new giant liners, the 30,000-ton *Lusitania* and the *Mauretania*, which were launched in 1906. For a short time these graceful four funnelled sister ships were the largest in the world, while for sheer speed they were without rivals for many years. The *Mauretania* won from the Germans the Blue Riband for the fastest Atlantic crossing and kept it safely for Britain for twenty-two years. She could average 25 knots for the journey, and both she and the *Lusitania* were the first ships to bring the two sides of the Atlantic within five days' sailing time of each other.

The Blue Riband holder was dwarfed by the 45,324-ton White Star liner *Olympic* on 1911, which was the world's biggest ship till she was overtaken by the *Titanic*. The *Titanic* displaced 46,000 tons and was hailed as the "unsinkable ship", a title that did not stop her from going down on her maiden voyage in 1912 when she ran full tilt into an iceberg. A 300-foot gash was torn in her side, and within hours the *Titanic* had disappeared forever beneath the waves, taking 1,503 of her passengers and crew with her to a watery grave. The inquiry into the accident revealed a scandalous state of affairs. Although the *Titanic* was licensed to carry a total of 3,547 people, there was room for only 1,178 of them in the lifeboats. As a result of the terrible loss of life, regulations were tightened, and, with luck, there will never again be a marine disaster of such frightening magnitude.

Britain's German rivals decided not to go for the sheer speed required for the Blue Riband, but to concentrate on their well-tried practice of combining luxury with great size. In the years immediately prior to World War I, the Germans built a succession of ships which surpassed all their predecessors in bulk. The 51,969-ton *Imperator* was launched in 1912, and the even larger *Vaterland* appeared in 1914, while the mighty 56,551-ton *Bismarck* was finished too late to go into service before the war started. When the conflict was over, the *Bismarck* came to Britain as compensation. She went to the White Star Line, and was renamed the *Majestic*.

World War I, which was at least partly due to the trading and maritime rivalry of Britain and Germany, saw few full-scale sea battles, though both countries had been building up their fleets for years. What the war did do was to bring several new types of naval vessels into prominence.

Undoubtedly, the major surprise of the war at sea was the shattering effectiveness of submarines. By early 1917 German *Unterseeboote* (U-boats) had brought Britain to the verge of defeat through starvation. One in every four merchant ships that sailed out of British ports was sunk. Convoys protected by naval destroyer escorts lessened the losses, but at one time there was only one month's supply of wheat in the entire country.

Submarines were not an invention of the twentieth century, though they did not really prove themselves until World War I. As long ago as James I's time, the Dutch inventor Cornelius Drebbel travelled underwater down the Thames from Westminster to Greenwich in a primitive submersible boat.

More advanced craft appeared in the eighteenth century, and during the American Revolution a submarine was first used for an underwater attack. In 1776 the *Turtle*, a one-man submarine built by the American David

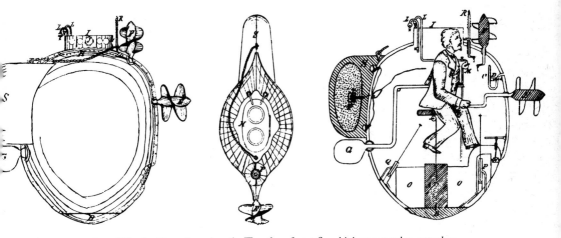

A reconstruction of Bushnell's submarine the Turtle *of 1776, which was used to attack a British warship during the War of Independence.*

Bushnell, moved stealthily below the waters of New York Harbour. Propelled by two hand-powered screws it crept beneath the anchored British flagship, *Eagle*, but an attempt to fix a time-fused charge was thwarted by the warship's tough copper sheathing. *Turtle* had to slip away with its half-hour supply of air exhausted, and all the British crew got was a severe fright when the gunpowder went off harmlessly.

A more refined device was designed in 1797 by Robert Fulton of steamboat fame. The *Nautilus*, as he called her, was launched in 1800. She was 123

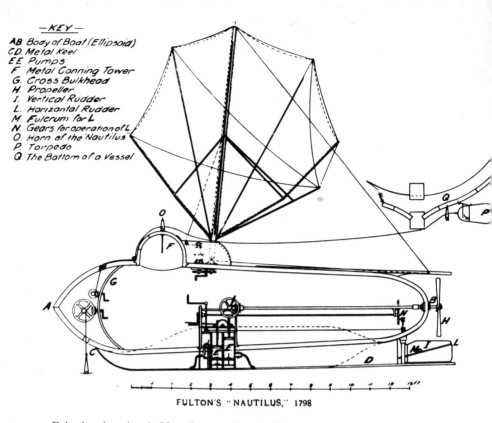

FULTON'S "NAUTILUS," 1798

Fulton's submarine the Nautilus *was launched in 1800. She was a great advance on Bushnell's design.*

built of steel and shaped like a long, narrow egg. Later Fulton rebuilt his submarine on Napoleon's orders, but the vessel was too successful for its own good, and the French refused to be responsible for the introduction of such a terrifying weapon. The British, who were doing very nicely at sea, could afford to be moral, and Fulton had no success with them either.

The development of submarines made little headway during the next sixty or seventy years because of the difficulty of propelling them underwater. Some inventors persisted with hand-driven vessels, and in 1864, during the American Civil War, a Confederate submarine of this kind managed to sink the Federal corvette *Housatonic*.

Mechanically driven underwater craft began to appear in the 1880's. A steam-driven submarine was demonstrated in 1880 by the English clergyman George Garrett, but since steam engines gobble up the air on which a submersible is dependent, long-distance dives were clearly out of the question.

More promising was the electrically driven boat planned by two more Englishmen, Campbell and Ash. Electric motors consume no air and are

The U.S. submarine Holland *was the model for later submersibles. She was purchased by the U.S. Navy in 1900.*

therefore ideal for use in submersible craft. The electric submarine was built for the inventors by Wolseley and Lyon in 1886. Its performance lived up to their hopes, except in one respect. The storage batteries of their day let them down. The batteries had to be recharged so frequently that the range of the submarine was limited to about eighty miles.

The use of electric motors was the clue that other inventors needed. The French conducted experiments during the 1890's, while in 1895 the American inventor John Philip Holland, after years of patient effort, at last secured an order for a submarine from the U.S. government. Holland's perfected design of 1898 featured a petrol engine for surface propulsion and electric motors for use under the sea.

Britain was the last of the great naval powers to introduce submarines. With overwhelming surface superiority, she had everything to lose and nothing to gain from their skulking, hidden method of attack. But by 1901 it had become clear that Britain could not stand aside and idly watch developments in other countries. Five Holland-type submarines were ordered for the Royal Navy. The first of these, which was only 60 feet long, was launched in October, 1901.

By 1914 Britain had built up her fleet of submarines to 60, while Germany possessed 38 U-boats. Realizing Britain's dependence on food and raw materials brought in by sea, the Germans worked furiously to produce more U-boats. During the war they made 300 submarines of all kinds and in the critical spring of 1917 used their new weapon to bring them within a hairs-breadth of victory.

The war hastened the development of another novel type of warship, the aircraft carrier. Initially, seaplanes were hoisted overboard to take off and land on the sea, but even prior to 1914 several nations had launched aircraft from small ship-mounted platforms. The first true aircraft carrier with an unobstructed flight deck for landing and taking off was H.M.S. *Argus*, the brainchild of the Royal Navy. She was converted from the Italian liner *Conte Rosso*, which was taken over during building. She displaced 14,000 tons, and her bow-to-stern flight deck extended for about 560 feet. The *Argus* was completed in 1918, but she was too late to see war service. She was the model for the carriers which played so important a part in later conflicts.

When Germany crumbled to defeat in 1918, the nations of the world could begin to count the cost of the war. Britain had lost 750,000 men, while France and Germany had each lost 1,500,000 men. Russian losses were probably greater than all the rest put together. Material destruction was colossal. At sea, Britain alone lost over 1,700 merchantmen by submarine attack in the last two years of the war. The world was never to recover from the shock of this titanic struggle.

Germany had to accept a humiliating peace treaty and almost complete disarmament. Her fleet was interned, and many of her prized liners were seized for war reparations. She was left in a mood of smouldering discontent which boded ill for the future.

It took years for the Germans to overcome the ravages of the war, but eventually her liners again began the challenge for the supremacy of the seas. The 50,000-ton *Bremen* was completed in 1929. She had two funnels, a modern look, and a turn of speed that enabled her to recapture the Blue Riband of the Atlantic for Germany after a lapse of more than twenty years. She could average nearly 28 knots for an Atlantic crossing, while the *Europa*, which followed a little later, was even faster.

These German successes spurred the British and French to build new giants of their own. The French answer was the *Normandie*, the first of the modern 1,000-foot liners, which made her maiden voyage in 1935. The

Normandie displaced something like 83,000 tons, and for some years was the

H.M.S. Argus, *the first aircraft carrier with an unobstructed flight deck, was completed in 1918. She is painted in the antisubmarine dazzle camouflage used in World War I.*

The Normandie, *perhaps the most beautiful transatlantic liner of them all, completed her maiden voyage in 1935.*

The giant Queen Elizabeth, *completed in 1940, was the younger of Cunard's two famous Queens. She was burnt out in Hong Kong harbour in January, 1972.*

The Queen Elizabeth II, *a successor to a famous name.*

biggest ship in the world. Many people think her the most beautiful transatlantic liner ever built, and without doubt, she was full of technical innovations. She was turboelectric, or, more explicitly, her four great propellers were driven by electric motors whose current came from steam-driven generators. This unorthodox power unit drove the *Normandie* across the Atlantic at an average speed of 31.2 knots to capture the coveted Blue Riband for France. Britain's own first 1,000-footer was the Cunard White Star liner *Queen Mary*, which was launched in 1934. In 1938 she beat the *Normandie*'s record by a fraction of a knot and reasserted Cunard's predominance on the North Atlantic. A third mighty ship, the *Queen Elizabeth*, the biggest of the three, was launched during the 1930's but did not make her debut till 1940, when she appeared in naval grey.

Less dramatic than the building of ocean giants, but nevertheless important

The British General, *a typical tanker of the 1920's.*

British Petroleum Tanker Company's British Admiral, *a modern 100,000-ton giant tanker.*

from the view of comfort and economy, was the gradual change from coal firing to fuel oil, which took place in the 1920's and 1930's. Fuel oil cut down by a striking extent the number of men needed in the stokehold. Before the Cunard liner *Aquitania* was converted to oil, she needed 350 stokers to satisfy her appetite for coal. After her refit, only 50 men were needed, and the ship was freed from coal dust and excessive smoke.

The use of oil in industry was increasing, and after World War I a larger number of tankers were built. The first modern steam tanker was made by the Armstrong Whitworth Company as long ago as 1886. She set the pattern, still followed today, of having her engine room right at the rear, well away from her inflammable cargo. Tankers remained comparative rarities, however, until the upsurge of motor traffic in the 1920's. By 1939 tankers constituted 16.9 percent of the world tonnage of merchant vessels.

World War II, which flared out of Germany's thwarted ambitions, again proved the striking power of the submarine. During the war years, 2,775 Allied and neutral merchantmen were sunk by submarine action.

More suprising was the vulnerability of even the biggest warships to aerial attack. The first hint of this came in 1940 with the assault by British Fleet Air Arm planes on the Italian fleet anchored at Taranto in southern Italy. The lesson was rammed home in 1941 by the treacherous, unprovoked raid of Japanese carrier-borne aircraft on the Americans at Pearl Harbour; in the space of an hour the Japanese sank four battleships and damaged many lesser vessels. The death knell of the battleship had been sounded, and by the end of the war, aircraft carriers had displaced them as the capital ships of the navies.

Since World War II the greatest shipbuilding activity has been concentrated on oil tankers. A typical oceangoing tanker of 1939 carried about 13,000 tons of oil. By the 1960's tankers capable of holding 100,000 tons were becoming commonplace, and even larger vessels were envisaged. The Japanese have become experts at building these giants and have even experimented with articulated models in an effort to make yet longer ships that would still withstand a storm without their backs being broken. By 1975 several Japanese-built tankers capable of carrying half a million tons of oil were in service.

Another postwar development has been in the use of new types of engines and fuels. Gas turbines give more power for less space and weight than steam units and have been installed in several vessels. The first to take to the sea was the 110-foot-long British motor gunboat 2009. This vessel had three screws, and in 1947 a 2,500-hp gas turbine was coupled to the central shaft. Since then other small ships have been powered by gas turbines, but progress is comparatively slow.

The British Navy has experimented with another unconventional engine, this time for use in submarines. One of the difficulties with powering a submarine has always been the need to conserve air when the vessel is submerged. The common solution to the problem was to use diesels on the surface and electric motors underwater. H.M.S. *Explorer*, which entered service in 1956, avoided the use of two sets of motors by employing hydrogen peroxide engines. Oxygen was released from the peroxide and used in the combustion of the fuel oil so that the valuable air supply would not be consumed by the engines. With its novel power system, the *Explorer* could run submerged for extended periods of time.

The most striking innovation has, of course, been in the use of nuclear energy at sea. Steam is raised by heat from a nuclear reaction and fed into

The U.S. submarine Nautilus *was the first vessel to be driven by nuclear power.*

a normal type of turbine. Since a little nuclear fuel will go a long way, the range of an atomic-powered ship is very great.

The first vessel with nuclear engines was the American submarine *Nautilus*, which was launched in 1954. She could keep up submerged speeds in excess of 20 knots for several weeks and proved so successful that a whole fleet of nuclear submarines was ordered. Some are always on patrol, lurking in the depths, with their nuclear missiles ready to retaliate for any surprise attack on the West. Perhaps the *Nautilus'* most famous exploit was her voyage under the polar ice to the North Pole in 1956. A still greater achievement was the eighty-three-day submerged circumnavigation of the globe by another American nuclear submarine, the *Triton*. Surface nuclear-powered vessels, like the U.S. merchantship *Savannah*, the U.S. aircraft carrier *Enterprise*, and the Russian icebreaker *Lenin*, have appeared since the

Savannah, *the first nuclear merchantship, was laid up in 1972 after ten years' service.*

Something new in transport. The original Saunders Roe SR-N 1 hovercraft crossing marshy ground.

Nautilus. Britain, too, has begun to build up a fleet of nuclear submarines, the first of which, the *Dreadnought*, was launched in 1960.

It is not only in fuels and motors that there have been changes. New methods of skating over the surface of the water have been invented. Hydrofoil boats of various kinds are used increasingly for carrying passengers on sheltered waters. Once in motion, these craft rise clear of the waves on what might be described as water wings. They can attain speeds nearly double those of ordinary boats.

Another device which leaves one wondering whether it is an aeroplane or a boat is the hovercraft. Work on this British invention began in the middle of 1958, and the Saunders Roe SR-N 1 made a number of "flights" over water, among them a Channel crossing in 1959. The new vehicle relies on the ground-cushion effect of a downward-directed jet of air acting between the water surface and the base of the hovercraft a short distance above. Since the machine skims over the surface without actually touching it, it can operate above reasonably smooth land, as well as sea. Commercial hovercraft services have been operated in several parts of the world, and hovercraft are being tested with the British and American armed forces. In 1966 cross-Channel services began to operate and hovercraft made the journey at something like 60 mph. The cut in transit time did much to gladden the hearts of the seasick. There seems to be a future for hovercraft on short passenger journeys like this one, but their wider use is still very much in question.

11

Man Gets His Wings: 1900–1920

The modern aeroplane is the child of the United States. While European inventors were still concentrating on becoming airborne, two American brothers, the Wrights, painstakingly worked out how to control a machine once it was in the air.

Wilbur (1867–1912) and Orville (1871–1948) Wright made their first man-carrying glider in 1900. It was a small, 17-foot wing-span biplane with only just enough lift to support a man. When completed, it was taken to the Kitty Hawk sand hills on the coast of North Carolina. The wind blew almost constantly over these exposed dunes, and their soft sands were ideal for cushioning heavy landings. Most of the time, the brothers flew their machine as a giant kite and controlled it with ropes from the ground. In this way they were able to test the elevators which made the glider climb or dive, but, more particularly, they were able to experiment on the effect of wing warping.

The Wrights had noticed that soaring birds could bank by twisting their wingtips, and they wanted to find out whether the same result could be achieved on a full-size glider. They made the wings flexible, so that they could be warped or twisted slightly during flight. It was found that if the trailing or rear edges of the wings on one side were twisted upward while at the same time the trailing edges on the other side were twisted downward, the first wings would drop, and the second wings would rise. The glider would tilt over to one side. Wing warping was a success and, for the first time, enabled a glider to be banked or righted if it began to tilt over accidentally. It was this control which gave the Wrights the advantage over all their rivals. Modern aeroplanes do not warp their wings; instead, they have hinging ailerons to make them bank. The basic idea, however, is still the same.

Once the controls had been proved, the brothers made a few piloted glides, but their machine was too small for satisfactory free flights and it had anyway served its purpose. As winter approached, they packed their bags and went home to build an enlarged version.

The Wrights' third glider being launched, 1902. Orville is at the controls.

The next year saw them back on the coast of North Carolina, this time at the Kill Devil Hills, some four miles from Kitty Hawk. Their second glider proved a failure. During wing warping it tended to slue around and sideslip into the ground. Evidently, more thought and research were needed.

A third glider appeared in 1902. It encountered the same trouble as its predecessor while banking, but this time the Wrights thought of a solution. They realized that the aircraft was sluing around because of the increased air resistance on one side when the rear edge of the wing was twisted downward. To compensate, they added a rudder to the back of the machine and linked it to the wing warping control. As the wings were twisted, the rudder was turned in order to correct the plane's tendency to slue around. Once this difficulty had been surmounted, the Wrights had at their disposal a thoroughly practical aeroplane, which would really respond to the wishes of the pilot. Between them they made more than 1,000 glides and became convinced that all they needed for sustained flight was a reliable light engine.

No suitable power plant was available, but the brothers were not to be beaten. They designed an engine of their own and installed it in a larger aircraft, modelled on their last successful glider. This machine, the *Flyer*, was completed toward the end of 1903. It was a biplane, like all its predecessors, but was well over twice the size of the first glider. The pilot lay across the middle of the lower wing, and the engine was mounted next to him on his right. Driving bands led from the engine to the two pusher propellers behind the wings. Struts stretched forward in front of the pilot to a biplane elevator, while further struts supported twin rudders at the rear of the machine. The undercarriage consisted of skids.

The trials were held on the Kill Devil sand dunes. By the morning of December 14, 1903, all was in readiness. A 60-foot launching rail had been laid down into the wind, and the *Flyer* was poised above it for takeoff. The brothers tossed a coin to decide who should go up first. Wilbur won and took his place across the wing. The engine was revved up and the tethering ropes cast off. With a roar, the machine charged down the launching rail and rose momentarily into the air, only to crash almost immediately into the soft sand. Even the imperturbable Wilbur had been excited enough to make a piloting error.

No great damage was done, but now it was Orville's turn. At about ten thirty on the morning of December 17, 1903, he took the *Flyer* along the same launching rail and climbed into the air for the first powered and controlled flight in history. It lasted only for 12 seconds, but those 12 seconds changed the world. Three more flights were made that day, and in the final one, Wilbur stayed up for 59 seconds.

The Wrights were not alone in their efforts of 1903. They had competition from other would-be aviators. One of these was the German, Jatho, whose semibiplane made uncontrolled hops covering up to 200 feet. Less successful was the American scientist Samuel Langley, whose earlier tandem-wing models had made promising flights of as much as 1,000 yards. His full-size aeroplane was, however, a complete failure. It was launched twice in 1903, with the engineer Charles Manly at the controls. On both occasions it crashed immediately, and the pilot was saved from injury only because the tests were carried out over water.

In 1904 the Wrights consolidated their success. A second *Flyer* was built, and the brothers continued to practise their new art. They made eighty short flights, during which they gradually mastered the difficult business of turning and circling. Their longest flight of this year lasted a little more than 5 minutes.

By now the Wrights had served their apprenticeship. Their third *Flyer*, built in 1905, was the world's first completely practicable aircraft. On her, the brothers could bank, turn, circle, and even fly in a figure eight, all with the greatest ease. Of the forty flights which they made in 1905, two lasted more than half an hour.

The Wrights' Flyer *makes the first powered and controlled flight, 1903.*

Europe's first officially recognized flight was not made until 1906, when Santos-Dumont persuaded his almost uncontrollable 14-bis to part company with the soil of France for a meagre 21.2 seconds. The peculiar-looking 14-bis had its biplane wings at the rear of its long, drooping body, so that in photographs it always seems to be flying backward.

It was not long, however, before Europe was producing machines which deserved to be called aeroplanes. In 1908 the Frenchman Louis Blériot built the world's first airworthy monoplane, while the biplane Voisin-Farman was, for its time, an outstanding aircraft. On January 13, 1908, the Voisin-Farman flew the first circle to be described in European skies and, shortly afterward, managed a flight lasting 45 minutes.

But these Continental achievements were completely overshadowed by Wilbur Wright's demonstration flights over France during the last half of 1908. A new *Flyer* was used, and Wilbur amazed everyone by his easy control over banks and turns. Lingering European scepticism about the Wrights' claims was swept aside, and the brothers were given the acclaim they richly deserved. Perhaps the greatest compliment they received was the speed with which the European pioneers adopted a control over banking. The grace and ease of Wilbur's turns had convinced all the experts that this kind of control was essential.

By October 1908, ailerons had been added to the successful Voisin-Farman. These wingtip flaps could hinge up or down, decreasing or increasing the lift of the wing as they did so. Ailerons produced the same banking effect as wing warping, and the Voisin-Farman example was followed by most European aircraft designers.

At this time Britain was a backwater nation as far as aviation was concerned. All the important events seemed to be occurring in America or in France. Even when a powered flight did at last take place over Britain in 1908, it was a gallant American, Colonel Cody, who was at the controls.

The most famous flight of 1909 was Blériot's Channel crossing. On July 25, he took off in one of his own monoplanes and headed out over the French coast across the forbidding grey waters of the English Channel. Half an hour

A famous moment in aeronautical history. The Frenchman Blériot crossing the English Channel.

later he was in England—and a world hero. There had been only one anxious moment, when the engine had spluttered in mid-Channel. Blériot's exploit captured the public imagination. Orders flooded in for his monoplanes, and so many were built that five years later, at the beginning of the First World War, some were still in military service.

While Blériot was preparing for the Channel flight, an impoverished young Englishman named A. V. Roe was experimenting with a triplane on the Lea Marshes, along the banks of London's second river. The only engine he could afford was a 9 hp motorcycle engine, so the underpowered machine had to be made as light as possible. To cut cost and weight, the wings were covered with brown paper. It was definitely a dry weather aeroplane. Despite all the difficulties, Roe coaxed his triplane into the air and became the first Briton to fly in an entirely British aircraft. Roe's flight was eclipsed by Blériot's achievement later in the same month, but fame came to the Englishman in the end. His firm later built some of the best known British aeroplanes of all time. To mention only a few, there was the time-defying Avro 504 of World War I, the illustrious Lancaster bomber which rained destruction on Nazi Germany, and the delta-winged Vulcan which is still serving with the Royal Air Force.

In August, 1909, a sort of aerial rally was held at Rheims, France. Thirty-eight machines were entered, and twenty-three actually took off to compete for the prizes. The American Glenn Curtiss took the speed prize in one of his own aeroplanes at 47 mph, the Englishman Hubert Latham rose to 500 feet to win the altitude award, and the Anglo-Frenchman Henri Farman set a new record by flying 112 miles without landing.

Rheims marked the end of the pioneering days of aircraft design. Man had proved he could fly; the task was now to improve performance and reliability, not just to stagger into the air. The improvements came with almost incredible speed.

The year 1910 was one of feverish activity. Aeroplanes flew in Germany, Switzerland, Russia, Belgium, and Holland. The air age was becoming international. New records were set. Speed increased to 68.2 mph, range to 363.3 miles, altitude record to 10,171 feet. The new capabilities of aircraft were dramatically proved by Chavez's crossing of the Alps, another triumphant first for a Blériot monoplane. Not so much noticed at the time, but nonetheless important, was the takeoff by a Curtiss biplane from a platform on the deck of the U.S. cruiser *Birmingham*. Also significant was the increasing military interest in flying. Even the cavalry-minded British Army introduced two Bristol Boxkite biplanes into the 1910 manœuvres on Salisbury plain.

138 The aeroplanes met with disapproval, though; they frightened the horses.

In 1909 A. V. Roe coaxed his triplane into the air and became the first Briton to fly in an entirely British aircraft.

But horses or no, the aeroplane was here to stay. In 1911 the Americans capped their deck takeoff with a successful landing on the U.S.S. *Pennsylvania*, and in Britain the world's first twin-engined plane, the Short Tandem-Twin, was built. On the Continent there was an increasing pre-occupation with military machines, so that by 1912 a reluctant Britain was practically forced to found her own Royal Flying Corps. The aeroplane was about to be used for a purpose very different from what the Wrights had ever intended.

The warplanes of 1914 were more dangerous to their pilots than to the enemy on the ground. No one had yet worked out how to use them as a lethal weapon, and reconnaissance was deemed to be their major function. When enemy aircraft met over the battlefront, the occupants usually just waved to one another.

These gentlemanly days did not last long. Pilots and observers began to carry revolvers and rifles. It relieved their feelings to fire a few shots but normally did little else. Bombs were also carried and dropped over the side

The first successful deck landing was made on the U.S. cruiser Pennsylvania *in 1911.*

Right: *A rare action shot of the German Fokker E monoplane of 1915. This little machine was the first true fighter plane.*

by hand. Naturally, such tiny missiles were more a nuisance than a serious inconvenience.

Air fighting became more dangerous when machine guns were generally adopted, but the whirling propeller got in the way and made it difficult and dangerous to shoot at an opponent. If the pilot were not careful, he could shoot himself down by blowing off his own propeller.

Serious aerial conflict dates from 1915, when the Dutchman Anthony Fokker produced an interrupter gear for the Germans. This device enabled a machine gun to be fired through the disk of a propeller without hitting the blades. Every time the propeller got in the way, the operation of the gun was automatically interrupted. Fokker fitted his invention to monoplanes of his own design and made indifferent machines into invincible killers.

British and French aircraft were helpless before this fierce little monoplane and fell in droves before its blazing guns. Allied pilots even thought of a new name for themselves, 'Fokker Fodder,' and for a while it seemed that the Germans would drive their demoralized enemies from the sky. The British answer was the pusher scout, which had its propeller at the rear of a short stubby body, instead of at the nose. With these machines, the pilot had a free forward field of fire. The "Fokker Menace" was checked, and time was gained for the Allies to bring in their own interrupter gear.

The little Fokker introduced the race of fighters to the air. After its success both sides strove to produce fighting scouts which could outmanœuvre, out-climb, outdistance, and outshoot all their opponents. The aim was to hamper reconnaissance, to discourage bombing, and, generally, to shoot the enemy out of the sky. The grim battle for air supremacy swayed first one way and then the other. Famous fighter planes were produced whose names have since become legendary. The British built their formidable Sopwith Camels, S.E.5's and twin-seat Bristol fighters; France had her redoubtable Nieuports and Spads; Germany had her sinister Fokker triplanes and graceful Albatrosses. Each technical advance by one side had to be countered by the other. The rate of progress in design was terrific.

Specially designed bombers were another child of the war. Fighters had to be small and speedy. They could not be built big enough to carry an effective bomb load. In the latter part of the war both sides were producing multi-engine bombers which could pack a lethal weight of high explosive. German Gothas became the scourge of London, and British Handley Pages made frequent unwelcome appearances over the Rhineland factories.

The typical aircraft of the World War I was the wooden-framed, fabric-covered biplane. Even 100-foot-wingspan bombers were usually made in the same fragile way. Wings had to be supported by struts and bracing wires, which added to the air resistance and slowed up the machines. The occasional monoplanes were also normally festooned with wire, so that their drag was almost as great as that of the biplanes and their speed, in consequence, not significantly higher.

The German firm of Hugo Junkers was almost alone in favouring the extensive use of metal in their aircraft. They pioneered the cantilever mono-plane wing, which was thick at the root and tapered as it extended toward the tip. Such wings needed no bracing wires to support them and were aerodynamically very clean. Professor Junkers' first all-steel monoplane of 1915 found no favour with the German authorities. Its unbraced wings seemed revolutionary and dangerous. Gradually, Junkers' ideas prevailed, and a steel and duralumin biplane, the J-1, saw service in the last years of

The S.E.5A was one of the most famous types of British fighters of World War I.

The German firm of Junkers pioneered metal aircraft. This Junkers J-1 was known as the "flying tank" to Allied pilots who encountered it in the closing stages of World War I.

the war. With its heavy armour, it was virtually a flying tank, and Allied airmen found it a very difficult machine to shoot down.

A year after the war, in 1919, a Junkers J-13 was operated by a German airline and so became the world's first all-metal civil aircraft. Junkers' designs were ahead of their time, however. Metal replaced wood for aircraft frames fairly rapidly, but fabric coverings remained general until the late 1920's.

12

Progress in Flight

When the war ended, military orders were cancelled. The hoped-for boom in civilian flying did not materialize, and the inflated aircraft industry collapsed. Many firms disappeared altogether. The public had yet to be convinced that air travel was fun. So the slow task began of building up the image of the aeroplane as a practical vehicle, not just the war-mount of adventurous young men.

Much was done even in 1919, the first full year of peace. The French Farman Lines opened the first international service and flew passengers between Paris and London in converted Goliath bombers. A few months later, British Air Transport and Travel Ltd., began the first daily services between the same cities. All over the Continent, major cities were linked by air routes, and bombers began to change their military drab for civilian silver.

The prestige of the aeroplane was further enhanced by two transatlantic crossings. First across was a Curtiss flying boat of the U.S. Navy which set out from Newfoundland in May, 1919, landed in the Azores, and then flew on to Lisbon. The first nonstop crossing followed in June, when the British fliers John Alcock and Arthur Brown coaxed their overloaded Vickers Vimy bomber off the ground, crossed the coast of Newfoundland, and headed east over a stormy Atlantic. They took off in the afternoon, flew through a tempestuous night during which ice formed on their wings and forced them to within fifty feet of the sea, and finally crash-landed in an Irish bog 16 hours after they had started. Both men were knighted by the King.

The Atlantic was also flown over in both directions during 1919 by the British airship R.34. Airships were a sort of blind alley in technical progress, but much effort and ingenuity went into their construction.

Before the First World War, Count von Zeppelin in Germany made a number of rigid airships, the seventh of which was actually put into passenger service in 1910. During the war years Zeppelins were used by the Germans for air raids and caused much alarm before it was discovered how easily

The American Curtiss flying boat NC-4 made the first transatlantic flight in 1919 but stopped to refuel in the Azores. Later in the same year, two Britons, Alcock and Brown, made a nonstop crossing.

they could be shot down by fighter planes. When peace came again, airships returned to passenger flying, and the comfort of their comparatively spacious cabins convinced many people that they were the mode of transportation of the future. A series of terrible accidents, which included the loss of the British R-101 in 1930 and which culminated in the destruction of the 803-foot-long German *Hindenburg* in 1937, put an end to hopes for giant airships. Today, dirigibles survive only as small nonrigid blimps that are inflated with inert helium gas instead of the dangerously inflammable hydrogen which was used to lift the earlier airships. Blimps are still used occasionally in the United States and elsewhere for aerial advertising.

Technical advances between the wars involved every facet of the aeroplane —construction, design, and engine. Structure changed from wooden frames with fabric covering, through metal frames with fabric surfaces, to genuine

The destruction of the German airship Hindenburg *in 1937 put an end to hopes for passenger dirigibles.*

all-metal aircraft made of the light alloy duralumin. High drag biplane designs began to give way to the cleaner and potentially faster monoplane. Improvements in engine efficiency and power enabled higher and higher speeds to be achieved.

Progress was not uniform. Although Junkers and Dutch Fokker monoplane airliners proved their worth on the Continent during the 1920's, Britain still persisted with large biplanes well into the 1930's. The strange thing was that these apparently clumsy British airliners were able to compare favourably with their rivals. They had reliability and a high standard of comfort. Passengers felt safe in them, and with good reason. The last eight Handley Page biplane airliners flew a total of 10,000,000 miles without a casualty. One was still flying in 1940.

148   *A Handley Page HP42 airliner of the 1930's. These large biplanes had admirable safety records.*

Charles Lindbergh taking off for the first solo flight across the Atlantic, 1927.

Military designs tended to lag behind civil progress. Britain and America were using biplane fighters until the late 1930's. Many of these were still fabric-covered, although in the mid-1920's metal frames had replaced wood. The first British fighter to show this change was the Siskin-111A of 1925. It was the same story with bombers; although monoplane bombers had long been available, a fabric-covered biplane bomber, the H. P. Heyford, was not retired from the Royal Air Force until 1939.

Yet the superiority of the monoplane was being proved beyond all doubt. Its reliability was demonstrated by the *Spirit of St. Louis* in which Charles Lindbergh made the first solo Atlantic crossing in 1927. Monoplane racers pushed the speed record up to values which no biplane could rival. Three successive wins in 1927, 1929, and 1931 by Supermarine monoplanes gave Britain permanent possession of the coveted Schneider Trophy for floatplanes. To cap this success, the final winner, the S.6B, set up a new speed record of 407·5 mph in 1931. Other superb monoplanes were coming in plenty. In 1934 the Italian Macchi MC-72 set a record of 440·7 mph which still stands for floatplanes, while in the same year the monoplane De Havilland Comet won the England to Australia race in a time of three days. Even more epoch-making were the American monoplane airliners which snatched civilian superiority from Europe in 1933. Until that year the United States, for all its technical resources, had contributed little to civil aviation. With the ten-seat Boeing 247 and the fourteen-seat Douglas DC-2, they made a great leap forward. Both were twin-engined, low-winged, all-metal monoplanes with retractable undercarriages, and both could fly at only a little less than 200 mph. They set a new trend in design.

149

With faster, safer, and more comfortable airliners, air travel gradually became more popular, but even in the 1930's most airlines needed to be supported by heavy government subsidies. Aircraft ranges were still limited, so that stages between refuelling stops could not be too long. Over land or across the island-strewn Pacific, this was not much of a problem, but the empty space of the Atlantic was for a long time an insurmountable barrier to passenger flights between the Old and the New Worlds.

As a pioneering step, the German airline Lufthansa adopted a daring scheme to get airmail to South America. In 1934 they anchored a depot ship in the South Atlantic to receive seaplanes flying out from the coast of Africa. The machines landed on the water and, after being hoisted aboard, were serviced and refuelled before being catapulted on their way to Brazil. This venture prospered, and in 1938 Lufthansa began to operate a similar service across the North Atlantic, using four-engined Blohm and Voss floatplanes.

The real honours went, however, to Britain and America. A British Empire Class flying boat of Imperial Airways and a Pan American Sikorsky S-42B boat made the first commercial crossings from different directions on the

A British Empire Class flying boat of the old Imperial Airways. In 1937 a boat of this kind shared the honour of making the first commercial crossing of the North Atlantic with a Pan American Sikorsky S-42B.

same day in 1937, the year before the German enterprise began. By 1939 the American company had begun to make crossings with passengers, but just as it seemed that the last great obstacle to airline flight had been conquered, the Second World War broke out. Civilian flying over Europe came to a halt.

Fortunately for the cause of freedom, the warlike preparations of Nazi Germany had frightened her neighbours into rearmament. British leaders favoured appeasement but had had enough sense to re-equip their air force. Monoplane fighters and bombers replaced the old-fashioned biplanes, and aircraft performance leaped by 100 mph. When Hitler launched his air fleet against southern England in 1940, he was met by a Royal Air Force, small in number, but great in quality. The Nazis were swept out of the sky by the superb new Spitfires and Hurricanes. The Battle of Britain was won, and Germany received her first reverse of the war.

In the tense years immediately prior to the outbreak of war, work was going on in secret to develop a new kind of engine. As soon as monoplanes began to top 300 mph, it became clear that propeller-driven aircraft were reaching the peak of their development. Certain farsighted engineers started to dream of an entirely new kind of power unit.

As long ago as 1928, while he was still a cadet in the Royal Air Force College, Sir Frank Whittle had written a thesis on jet propulsion. By 1937 he had translated theory into reality, and was running a jet engine on the test bench. Meanwhile, others were working on the same idea in Germany. With backing from the warlike Nazi regime, the Germans made rapid progress. On August 27, 1939, they were able to put the Heinkel He 178 into the air for the world's first jet flight. This first jet could reach 435 mph. Its immediate successor, the twin jet Heinkel He 280, which flew in 1941, could achieve well over 550 mph. Fortunately, Whittle's research was by this time bearing fruit, and a British jet was ready to fly. On May 15, 1941, the Gloster E.28/39 took off under the power of a Whittle W-1 turbojet. This little machine is of great historical interest. It is the ancestor of all British and American jets, because during the war both countries pooled their researches on this topic. The first American jet plane, the Bell Airacomet, followed in 1942.

Gradually, but inexorably, the tide of war turned against the Axis Powers. British and American long-range bombers battered German cities and smashed war factories. In a desperate effort to stem this flood of destruction, the Nazis evolved jet and rocket fighters of startlingly advanced design. The use of the twin-jet Messerschmitt Me 262 and the sweptwing rocket-propelled Me 163 against Allied bomber formations in 1944 came as an 151

The brilliant twin-jet Messerschmitt Me 262. But for production delays it might have halted American daylight attacks on Germany in 1944.

The Gloster E.28/39 was the first British jet to fly, May 15, 1941.

unpleasant shock, but by then Germany was doomed. Not even the use of Hitler's vengeance weapons, the V-1 and the V-2, could save her.

These devices were among the greatest examples of misplaced human ingenuity to come out of the war. The V-1 was a jet-propelled flying bomb which could carry 1,870 pounds of explosives for 150 miles, at speeds approaching 400 mph. The V-2 was a rocket bomb which travelled at 3,600 mph and rose to 60 miles before plunging down on its target. Fortunately, spies warned the Allies of German preparations, and an air onslaught was mounted against launching sites and research centres. As a result, the Nazis were never able to devastate London and southern England, as they had hoped. Nevertheless, during 1944 about 8,000 V-1's were fired against England, and those that avoided the fighters and anti-aircraft guns killed more than 6,000 people. V-2's were never fired in anything like that quantity, but they were weapons of crucial significance. Once fired, they could not be intercepted. They foreshadowed the space age and the ballistic missile.

The Allies were so successful with their conventional aircraft that they had little incentive to adopt daring new designs. Despite all the Nazi efforts, German cities continued to be bombed night and day. Only one type of Allied jet aircraft was put into action. That was the British twin-engine Gloster Meteor, which was used to shoot down V-1's in 1944.

Jets and rockets took the headlines, but they were not the only technical

The Gloster Meteor was the only Allied jet to see action in World War II.

advances to be perfected under the pressure of war. By the time the conflict ended, the United States and Germany had also mastered the art of hovering flight and vertical takeoff and landing. They had both produced practicable operable helicopters.

The helicopter has a long history. Leonardo da Vinci designed one, models were flown in the eighteenth and nineteenth centuries, and in the early twentieth century many attempts were made to build full-size man-carrying machines. None of the inventors had any real success with these large rotorcraft until the Spaniard Juan Cierva came on the scene in 1923 with an aircraft which he called an autogiro.

The original autogiro had a large four-bladed rotor mounted above the fuselage but, aside from that, looked fairly similar to a normal aeroplane. It had short, stubby wings and a propeller mounted at its nose. The rotor was not connected to the engine as it is in the modern helicopter. To take off, the machine taxied forward. The rotor began to windmill in the airstream and so lifted the aircraft into the air.

Cierva's autogiros had one great defect. They could not hover over one spot and still hold their height. For this, a helicopter with a power-operated rotor was needed. Louis Bréguet in France had a partial success in 1935 with a machine which could stay airborne for an hour and achieve a speed of 30 mph, but the German twin-rotor Focke-Achgelis Fa 61 of 1936 was the first helicopter that could be controlled properly. It was flown extensively until the war, and the accumulated experience was used in the design of the Focke-Achgelis Fa 223, which appeared in 1940. The Fa 223 was put into production and was used during the last two years of the war to supply isolated units of the German Army.

The work of the Russian immigrant Igor Sikorsky in the United States was, however, of much more lasting importance. It was he, more than any other person, who made the helicopter industry what it is today. His first successful rotorcraft was the VS-300, which flew on September 14, 1939. Unlike its German rivals, it had only one lifting rotor, though a stabilizing propeller was mounted sideways at the very end of the fuselage to prevent the body from twisting around in flight. Sikorsky's experiments led up to the the R-4B, which was ordered into large-scale production in 1944.

Though they were too late to make a major contribution to the war, helicopters soon proved themselves in peacetime. They could fly forward or backward by tilting their rotors in the appropriate direction, they could hang motionless above a given spot, and they could land and take off vertically. Their versatility has made them a common sight the world over.

154 The other great aeronautical development of the war, the jet engine,

A Cierva autogiro being tested in 1926.

Sikorsky's first successful helicopter, the VS-300, first flew in September, 1939. Sikorsky did more than any other man to establish the helicopter industry.

took a little longer to make its full impact on civilian flying, but it was taken up by the world's air forces with great enthusiasm. Jet fighters soon replaced the much slower piston-engine types in all the major air forces, but propeller-driven bombers, with their longer range, survived right into the 1950's.

Speeds increased spectacularly. On November 7, 1945, a few months after the end of the war, a British Gloster Meteor established a new record of 606·38 mph. About two years later, an American, Major Charles Yeager, became the first man to fly faster than the speed of sound. His research aircraft, the Bell X-1, was lifted to a height of 30,000 feet by a Boeing Superfortress and then released. The major opened up his rocket engines and thrust his machine through the thin, cold air at 700 mph, faster than sound could travel at that height.

By the early 1950's many fighters could break the sound barrier in shallow dives, and sonic booms became a standard part of the entertainment at air displays. It was not until October, 1953, however, that an operational

The American Douglas DC-2 was a great leap forward in airliner design.

fighter, the North American F-100 Super Sabre, managed to exceed the speed of sound in level flight. Only seven years later the U.S. Air Force brought a supersonic bomber, the B-58 Hustler, into service, while today fighters like the Russian MiG-23 can fly at 2,100 mph.

Britain was the pioneer of civilian jet flying. On May 2, 1952, a De Havilland Comet of B.O.A.C. took off from London for Johannesburg to inaugurate the world's first scheduled jet passenger service. The Comets quickly became the most popular machines on the airline routes, and Britain seemed years ahead of her competitors. Then came a series of inexplicable disasters, which led to the Comets being grounded in 1954. Wreckage from one crash was dredged up from the floor of the Mediterranean, and scientists managed to trace the fault to a previously almost unknown kind of metal fatigue. Eventually a modified Comet flew again, but precious time had been lost, and Britain never regained her lead in jet transport.

In 1952 the Comet 1 became the first jet airliner to enter service. A tragic sequence of accidents later marred its success.

The pure jet was not the only new type of power unit. Turboprop engines, which used both propellers and the thrust of hot exhaust gases, had been developed at about the same time and proved highly efficient and economical in their use of fuel. Britain was a pioneer in this field, too, and produced the world's first operable turboprop airliner, the Vickers Viscount. This time there was no tragic sequel. From the moment she went into service in 1953, the Viscount has been an outstanding success.

Turboprops and, more especially, jets, give the high speeds that modern passengers seem to demand. Since about 1960 no new major airliner has been designed which does not use engines of one or the other of these types. Older piston-driven machines still give good service off the prestige routes, but it is clear that the day of petrol-engine airliners is nearing its end.

Already, big jets, like the Boeing 747 and the Vickers VC-10, cross the Atlantic at speeds approaching 600 mph, but still the quest for more speed goes on. Britain and France have combined to build the supersonic Concorde, which on entering airline service in 1976 should slash the flying time between London and New York to less than $3\frac{1}{2}$ hours. Russia's challenger, the Tu-144, is slightly faster, but has run into development difficulties.

Concorde has a long-range cruising speed of 1,350 mph.

The Tu-144 has been much modified since this early prototype first flew.

As flying speeds have increased, runways have had to be lengthened. Modern high-performance aeroplanes are limited to specially prepared airfields. From a military point of view, this is a great disadvantage. Aeroplanes are needed in the fighting area, not miles back on their long stretches of immaculate concrete. The ideal military aircraft should be able to operate from virtually any level site. Designers have tried several methods of coping with this difficulty.

One solution is to make a high-speed machine capable of taking off vertically. This can be done in a number of ways. An early idea was the tail sitter, the first example of which was the American Convair XFY-1 of 1954. This sat on its tail for takeoff and pointed vertically into the sky. Its propeller acted like a helicopter rotor and lifted the aircraft to a good height before it tilted over and used its delta wings to sustain it in the air in the normal way.

The Rolls-Royce Flying Bedstead of the same year was entirely different. It raised itself by the vertical thrust of two jet engines. Actually, this machine was not a real aeroplane at all but was merely a hovering test rig intended to explore the problems of controlling vertical takeoff. These experiments were followed up by the delta-winged Short SC-1, which had four jets to provide vertical lift and another one for use in ordinary flight. The SC-1 achieved its first vertical takeoffs in 1958.

The most successful vertical takeoff aircraft to date is the Hawker-Siddeley Harrier, a ground attack fighter serving with the RAF and the US Marine Corps. This machine uses yet another technique to become airborne. Thrust from its jet is deflected downward, so that the airplane is lifted into the air. Slowly, the deflection of the jet blast is reduced. The Harrier begins to pick up horizontal speed and moves faster and faster until finally all the force of the jet is used for forward propulsion, and the wings alone supply lift.

An early vertical takeoff and land aircraft, the U.S. Convair XFY-1 of 1954.
It was designed to take off and land on its tail.

Vertical takeoff has been one line of thought for military designers. Another idea is the variable-incidence wing, which can be extended straight out for low-speed landings, but be swept back while actually in flight in order to allow the machine to achieve a high performance in action. The United States, the Soviet Union, and France have all developed variable-geometry fighters.

Flying machines have certainly progressed in the seventy-odd years since the time of the Wrights. Jets scream across the sky faster than their sound can follow them; fighters jump vertically into the air before streaking off to their targets; helicopters hang poised beneath their whirling rotors. The air has almost been tamed, and already man is stretching out toward new adventures beyond his own shallow atmosphere.

Above, opposite: The Hawker Siddeley Harrier. A VTOL aircraft in service with the RAF and US Marine Corps.

Bottom, opposite: The American F-111, pioneer variable geometry aircraft.

The F-100 Super Sabre, the first operational fighter to fly faster than the speed of sound in level flight.

13

The Conquest of Space

German World War II V-2 missiles, which hurtled to a height of 60 miles before plunging onto their targets, carried their explosive warheads to the very verge of space. At the end of the war the Americans and probably the Russians, too, seized a number of these rockets before the Germans had time to fire them. The United States altered its captured V-2's so that they could climb vertically, instead of following a curved path toward some distant objective. Scientific instruments were fired higher than ever before, enabling the study of the upper layers of the atmosphere. In 1946 one of the modified rockets rose to a height of 116 miles.

To reach even greater heights, the United States mounted a tiny 16-foot-long second stage rocket on the nose of a V-2. When the main rocket reached its maximum height, the smaller one ignited and climbed even higher. Eight such firings were made between 1948 and 1950, and in 1949 a second-stage rocket rose to 242 miles while its instruments transmitted data back to earth.

During the 1950's both the United States and the Soviet Union poured vast amounts of money into the development of war rockets. The original V-2 had a maximum range of 230 miles. Its descendants in the 1950's could carry H-bombs to targets thousands of miles away and rise to heights of about 600 miles. These weapons of destruction were to become the tools used to put man into space.

Crucial developments occurred during the 1957-58 International Geophysical Year, which was held so that scientists of all nations could learn together as much as possible about the earth and its atmosphere. Salvos of research rockets were sent soaring into the sky to probe the secrets of the earth's upper atmosphere. The greatest sensation of the year was the Soviet Union's launching of the world's first artificial satellite. Sputnik I, as the Russians called it, was sent into orbit on October 4, 1957. It was a metal sphere 23 inches in diameter and weighed 184·3 pounds. During the first part of its 1,400-orbit flight, it radioed back information about the density

A German V-2 rocket missile being launched. The development of these weapons toward the end of World War II marked the beginning of the space age.

and temperature of the rarefied atmosphere through which it was travelling. Gradually, as it spiralled lower, it began to heat up by friction with denser layers of air. Sputnik I finally burned out on January 4, 1958.

Sputnik II was fired into orbit on November 3, 1957. It was a massive satellite weighing half a ton and carried inside it the first space traveller, the mongrel bitch Laika. The dog stayed alive for seven days, during which time her reactions were relayed down to earth. No means had yet been developed for recovering satellites from space, so Laika had to be sacrificed to the cause of science. Sputnik II orbited at heights of between 140 miles and 1,038 miles and made about 2,370 circuits of the world before it burned up on April 14, 1958.

The United States, was, at first, very unlucky with its satellite program. Time after time, launchings went wrong, and rockets were destroyed on the launching pad. Eventually the United States, too, succeeded, and on January 31, 1958, it sent the world's third artificial satellite, Explorer I, into orbit. Explorer was tiny in comparison with the Russian giants. It weighed only 30·8 pounds compared to Sputnik II's half a ton, an indication of the vastly superior power of the Soviet rockets at that time.

What the American satellites lacked in size, they made up for in the sophistication of their instruments. The United States' Vanguard satellite, launched on March 17, 1958, discovered, for instance, that the world is slightly pear-shaped, with the smaller end at the North Pole. Vanguard climbed so high that it will probably stay in orbit for several centuries.

Since these early launchings, hundreds of satellites and probes have been fired. Most have orbited our own earth, gathering information from the borders of space, but some have left the world behind to pry into the secrets of the solar sytem.

In 1959 the Soviet Union made some notable moon shots. Lunik I was launched in January and passed within 3,700 miles of the moon before going into orbit around the sun. Lunik II scored a hit on the moon surface in September, while in the next month Lunik III photographed the hidden side of the moon and relayed its pictures back to earth.

Other probes have gone even further. America's Mariner II passed within 22,000 miles of Venus in 1962 and radioed back much information on the planet's characteristics. Since this first successful interplanetary probe the Russian Venera series has contributed still more to our knowledge of Venus. Capsules, parachuted down through the planet's swirling clouds, have recorded temperatures as high as 500°C.

Venus has not been the only planet to receive attention. Mariner IV flew past Mars in July, 1965, and took a sequence of twenty-one pictures,

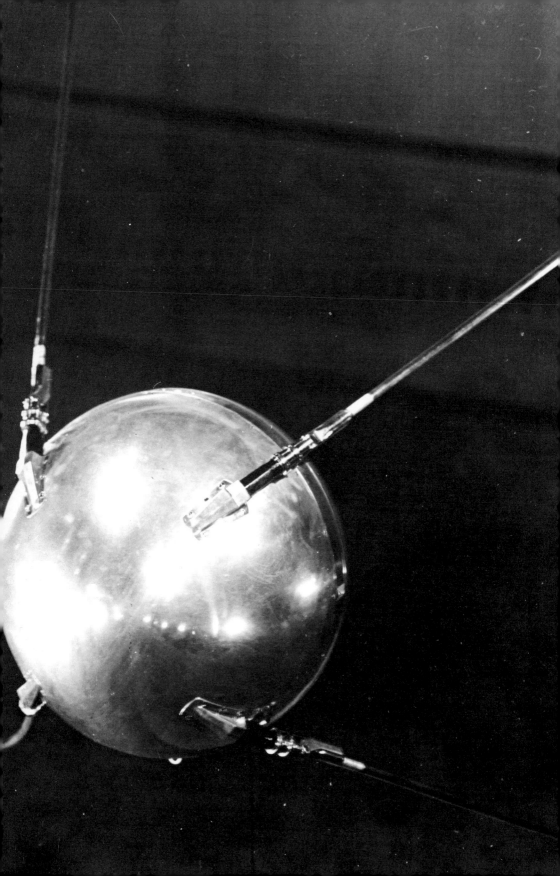

the closest at a height of a little more than 6,000 miles. Mariners VI and VII continued the process of exploration and penetrated even closer, but it was Mariner IX which first succeeded in mapping a large proportion of the planet's surface from an orbital vantage point into which it was injected in November, 1971. March, 1972, saw the United States launch a probe which passed within 81,000 miles of Jupiter on 3 December, 1973, sending back striking pictures of this giant of the planetary system.

In 1966 the Soviet Union and then the United States succeeded in soft-landing unmanned spacecraft on the moon. Neither ship was swallowed up in enveloping dust, as some scientists had feared, and both radioed back excellent pictures of the lunar surface.

The unmanned satellites and probes first paved the way for and then supplemented the research efforts of piloted space vehicles. Before men could venture into space, the effects of radiation and micrometeoroid bombardment had to be investigated, while the problem of re-entering the atmosphere without burning up also had to be overcome.

A step toward conquering the re-entry problem was taken in August, 1957, when a small nose cone from an American Jupiter missile was recovered from the Atlantic after a climb to 270 miles and a plunge toward earth at 9,000 mph. In May, 1958 a full-size nose cone was safely retrieved after a similar experiment, but later in the year there was a setback. A chimpanzee made a successful 1,700-mile missile flight, only to drown after his nose cone had splashed down in the South Atlantic.

Manned space flights were brought still nearer, when, in May, 1959, two monkeys survived a 1,500-mile flight from the United States launching base in Florida and were successfully rescued from the sea. Two more monkeys and a chimpanzee lived through further tests, and none of the animals showed any sign of harmful after-effects.

The Russians had begun to fire animals to high altitudes in the early 1950's in order to study their reactions to weightlessness and rapid acceleration. Later they expanded their research with animals in preparation for piloted orbital flights. In July, 1959, two Soviet dogs were brought down safely after a rocket flight to a great height. The breakthrough came, however, in August, 1960, when a Soviet spaceship containing two dogs and other animals and plants was successfully recovered after orbiting the earth for 25 hours. The re-entry problem had been solved. Spaceships could be brought back into the denser lower atmosphere without frying their occupants. Better still, none of the animals or plants was injured by radiation during 169

Yuri Gagarin's spacecraft, Vostok I, April, 1961.

their journey through space. Other dogs were put into orbit and brought back unharmed in 1961. It was time for man himself to venture forth.

The first man to go into space was the Russian Major Yuri Gagarin. On April 12, 1961, he was launched in the spaceship Vostok I. Vostok I reached a maximum height of 203·5 miles and, in a period of 108 minutes, made just over one circuit of the earth before re-entering the atmosphere. Yuri Gagarin, looking down through a small porthole, had the first space view of earth. He was struck then, like all the other astronauts who came after him, by the limpid blue of the planet below.

The United States was not yet ready for a full orbit of the earth. Its first astronaut, U.S. Navy Commander Alan Shepard, had to be content with a short testing flight. On May 5, 1961, his Mercury capsule was fired to a height of 116·5 miles and splashed down in the sea 302 miles from the launching site.

On August 6, 1961, the Soviet Union launched a second astronaut into orbit. Major Gherman Titov, on board Vostok II, stayed in space for about twenty-five hours and made seventeen orbits of the world. Five thousand

The Mercury capsule, Freedom-7, in which Commander Alan Shepard made America's first space flight, May, 1961.

miles from the chosen landing area, the ground command operated Vostok's retro-rockets. The satellite's speed was checked, and it began its plunge through the lower atmosphere. At 20,000 feet, Titov was ejected from the capsule and descended safely by parachute onto Russian soil. The Russians do not favour the American technique of splashdown in the ocean.

By now the United States was dipping deep into its immense fund of engineering knowledge in a tremendous effort to catch up on the Soviet lead. On February 20, 1962, Lieutenant Colonel John Glenn of the United States Marine Corps became the first American to orbit the earth. An Atlas missile blasted his Mercury capsule into orbit at 17,500 mph. After a flight of about five hours and three circuits of the world, the retro-rockets were ignited. The spaceship slowed slightly and dipped for its final blazing rush through the lower atmosphere. As it hurtled into ever denser layers of air, friction slowed it still further and heated it to furnace conditions. The heat shield in front of the capsule glowed white-hot at 3,000°F., but inside the insulated cabin the temperature stayed below 100°F. At 30,000 feet a parachute opened, and the spaceship floated gently down into the Caribbean Sea, where a fleet of rescue boats was waiting.

The sequence of one-man Mercury flights was successfully continued, and each orbit gained fresh information. Lieutenant Commander Scott Carpenter made three orbits in May, 1962. His colleague Walter Schirra completed five circuits in October. In May, 1963, Major Gordon Cooper of the U.S. Air Force was launched on America's first really long space flight of twenty complete orbits of the world.

Meanwhile, the Russians were still ahead in manned orbital flight. On August 11, 1962, Major Andrian Nikolayev was launched in Vostok III. Vostok IV, with Lieutenant Colonel Pavel Popovich on board, followed a day later. So accurately had their orbits been controlled that the two capsules passed within three miles of each other. The pilots were able to test radio communication between spaceships in flight. With manual controls, they could have manœuvred even closer. The possibility of rendezvous in space was proved.

Ten months later a similar experiment involved the first woman astronaut. Vostok V was put into orbit on June 14, 1963, with Lieutenant Colonel Valery Bykovsky on board. Vostok VI, containing Miss Valentina Tereshkova, followed two days later. Again, the two ships closed to within three miles, and the pilots experimented with intership communication.

For prolonged flights or voyages away from the earth, larger space vehicles are needed. Late in 1964, the Soviet Union put Voskhod I into orbit, with a crew of three aboard. Four and a half months later, on March 18,

The first American to walk in space. Astronaut Edward White clambered out of Gemini IV during its third orbit, June, 1965.

1965, Colonel Pavel Belyayev and Lieutenant Colonel Aleksei Leonov made seventeen orbits in Voskhod II. During the flight Leonov crawled through an airlock and launched himself into space. His only contact with the ship was the cable which pumped life-giving oxygen into his helmeted suit. He whirled along beside the Voskhod, a tiny living satellite of the earth and was the first human being to walk in space.

Later, in March, 1965, while Colonel Belyayev and Lieutenant Colonel Leonov were being welcomed back in Moscow, the United States launched its first Gemini, with astronauts Virgil Grissom and John Young on board.

The two-man Gemini was an important step forward in the American plan to land men on the moon. From the moment in 1961, when the late President John F. Kennedy authorized a moon exploration programme, each manned space flight undertaken by the United States was designed to make its own definite contribution towards the ultimate goal.

There had been fears of health hazards from prolonged periods of weight-lessness. Astronauts were sent up to find out whether these fears had any basis. Gordon Cooper and Charles Conrad stayed up for eight days in Gemini V during August, 1965, while in December of that year Frank Borman and James Lovell were aloft for fourteen days in Gemini VII. Neither crew came to any harm, and one worry could be discarded.

Repairs might be necessary in space. The technique was investigated by James McDivitt and Edward White during their four-day orbital flight aboard Gemini IV in June, 1965. Early in the mission White climbed out of the spacecraft and became the first American to walk in space. Propelling himself with a gas gun and by tugs on the oxygen hose, which was his only connection with the ship, he enjoyed his twenty-minute jaunt so much that he was reluctant to go back inside.

Eleven days after Gemini VII's long flight had begun in December, 1965, her sister ship, Gemini VI, was sent up to rendezvous with her. Schirra and Thomas Stafford managed to bring Gemini VI within a few feet of their target, and the two craft manœuvred around each other while their crews took some amazing photographs of spaceships in flight. Gemini's control system was proved beyond doubt.

In July, 1966, Gemini X achieved a trouble-free docking with an un-manned Agena rocket, which had been parked in orbit. The mastery of this technique was crucial to further progress, since the Apollo moon shot was to involve two docking operations.

The Apollo plans, published in 1962, revealed that the moon landing was to be attempted in a light descent vehicle which had subsequently to rise and reunite with an orbiting command ship. At the time this decision seemed daring, but in the event the planners' judgement was completely vindicated. When Apollo 11 took its 'giant leap for mankind', it was carrying into practice what had been meticulously thought out years before.

The typical Apollo flight began with the spacecraft being put into earth orbit while still attached to the third stage of the giant Saturn V launch vehicle. Computers on the ground then worked out the exact moment at which the third stage should be reignited to send it on a trajectory towards the moon.

With this second firing accomplished, the astronauts had to initiate one of the most difficult manoeuvres of the whole operation. The already linked command module (CM), housing the crew of three, and service module (SM), containing fuel supplies, had to be coupled to the lunar excursion module (LM), tucked away in a protective adapter between them and the third stage. A short burst on the SM engines pushed the combined command

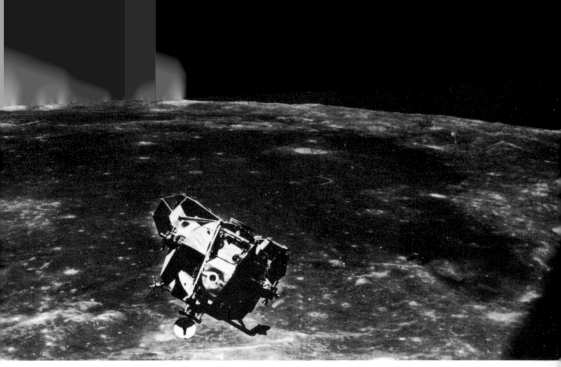

The ascent module nears the Apollo 11 command ship after man's first landing on the moon.

The recovery of the Apollo 11 command module after splashdown in the Pacific.

and service modules (CS M) free, and as they broke away the metal plates enclosing the lunar module were blown off. The CS M had then to be turned and brought back to dock nose to nose with the L M. At this point spring thrusters detached the spent third stage, leaving the completed Apollo assembly to coast on for the moon.

Sixty-six hours later as the Apollo neared its target, ground control activated the main engine of the SM to put the spacecraft into orbit around the moon. Further firings adjusted the orbit to a height from which the two-man lunar module could be launched to make the final descent.

After a day or more on the moon's surface the astronauts took off in the upper portion of the LM, using the lower part as a launching platform. Their lightened craft soared into orbit, sought out the command module, and docked. Once the members of the landing party had rejoined their colleague inside the main ship, the ascent module was discarded. The SM motor was opened up and Apollo headed for home.

Such a complex sequence could not be mastered without a series of manned proving flights. The first of these was scheduled for February, 1967, but tragically never took place. With less than a month to go the crew were killed when a fire gutted their command module during a practice session.

Extensive modifications held back the next manned attempt until October, 1968. This time, however, all went well, and Apollo 7 returned safely from an eleven-day earth-orbital flight. With confidence restored, the way was cleared for more ambitious missions.

Apollo 8 flew to the moon in December, 1968 and achieved lunar orbit. Apollo 9 was launched into earth orbit in March, 1969 to practise docking manoeuvres. Apollo 10 was entrusted with the final rehearsal. In May, 1969, its crew were given the frustrating task of carrying through the entire sequence, stopping short only at the actual lunar landing. Now all was ready for the 'big one'.

Apollo 11, with Neil Armstrong as commander, Michael Collins as command module pilot, and Edwin Aldrin as lunar module pilot, was launched from Cape Kennedy on July 16, 1969. Four days later the lunar module was sitting safely on the moon's surface, while its two occupants struggled into their special protective suits. Armstrong, as commander, was first to venture out. To him fell the honour of planting the first human footstep on an extra-terrestrial soil.

Five further Apollo missions have been sent to the moon and only one, Apollo 13, has run into such serious difficulties that the lunar landing has

Right: *The Saturn V rocket, the power unit of the American moon project. Compare the size with ringed figure of man on right.*

The lunar rover taken to the moon by Apollo 15 in July, 1971, greatly increased the astronauts' mobility.

had to be abandoned. The years of patient research and development have paid off. Knowledge concerning the moon has been vastly increased.

Soviet efforts at lunar exploration have so far been limited to such ingenious remote controlled spacecraft as Luna 16, launched in September 1970, which succeeded in scooping up a small sample of moon dust and bringing it home. The Luna series has continued over the years, number twenty-three was launched in 1974, and although the programme lacks the glamour of Apollo it must rank as a technical achievement of the highest order.

Russia has also pressed on with manned orbital flights though not without tragic setbacks. The Soyuz series, aimed at establishing an orbital laboratory, has been dogged with bad luck. In 1967 the first manned Soyuz mission terminated with the death of the pilot when the capsule's re-entry parachutes failed. All went well for some years then misfortune struck again. After successfully docking with an unmanned Salyut space station, Soyuz 11 suffered a sudden depressurization on re-entering the atmosphere. The crew of three were killed. Modifications were made and since then the programme has prospered. In July 1975 a Soviet Soyuz and an American Apollo rendezvoused and docked with one another in a much heralded act of international co-operation in space. Perhaps the perspective of space-flight, which shows the earth for what it is, a tiny speck in the vastness of the solar system, will at last persuade mankind to work together for the good of its planet.

Acknowledgements

Acknowledgements are due to the following for permission to reproduce pictures on the pages indicated: Associated Press Ltd, 147; British Aircraft Corporation, 159 (top); British Hovercraft Corporation, 132; British Motor Corporation, 110, 111, 114 (top); British Museum, 7, 14, 17, 20, 21, 29 (top), 31, 32, 42, 52; British Overseas Airways Corporation, 150, 158; British Petroleum Company Ltd., 129 (bottom); George Clark & N.E.M. Ltd., 94 (bottom); Cunard Steam-Ship Company Ltd., 121 (top), 128; Curtiss-Wright, 146; Filmstelle der Deutschen Bundesbahn, 117; Ford Motor Company Ltd., 107, 114 (bottom right); French Line, 127 (bottom); Friends of Canterbury Cathedral, 34; General Motors Corporation, 110 (bottom), 113; General Post Office, 50; Handley Page Ltd., 148; Hawker-Siddeley Ltd., 118, 162 (top); Illustrated London News, 91, 93; Imperial War Museum, 127 (top), 141, 143, 152, 153, 166; Japan Information Centre, 116; Charles E. Lee, 41; McDonnell Douglas Corporation, 157; Mercedes-Benz Ltd., 78 (right); National Maritime Museum, 27, 29 (bottom), 59; Norton Villiers Ltd., 114 (bottom left); Novosti Press Agency, 159 (bottom), 168, 170; Radio Times Hulton Picture Library, 46, 155; Rolls-Royce Ltd., 106; Rover Company Ltd., 112; Royal Army Corps Tank Museum, 109; Science Museum, 1, 3, 4, 5, 6, 10, 13, 16, 18, 19, 35, 37, 39, 40, 44, 48, 54, 56, 57, 62, 64, 65 (top), 67, 69, 70, 72 (right), 76, 77, 78 (left), 81, 83, 84 (top), 88, 94 (top), 96, 97, 98, 100, 102, 103, 121 (bottom), 129 (top), 134, 139; Sikorsky Aircraft, 156; Société Bertin, 119; Thames & Hudson Ltd., 9; Union Pacific Railroad Museum, 74 (bottom); United States Information Service, 38, 65 (bottom), 72 (left), 74 (top), 84 (bottom), 85, 99, 123, 124, 125, 131, 136, 137, 140, 149, 161, 162 (bottom), 164, 171, 173, 175, 177, 178; Universitetets Oldsaksamling, Oslo, 23, 21.

Index of Craft and Models

Bold figures refer to illustrations

General Index

Bold figures refer to illustrations